THE NORTH AMERICAN
MARIA THUN
BIODYNAMIC
ALMANAC
2020

CREATED BY
MARIA AND MATTHIAS THUN

Floris
Books

Compiled by Matthias Thun
Translated by Bernard Jarman
Additional astronomical material
by Wolfgang Held and Christian Maclean

Published in German under the title *Aussaattage*
English edition published by Floris Books

British Library CIP Data available

ISBN 978-178250-605-8
ISSN: 2052-577X

Printed in Poland through Hussar

Floris Books supports sustainable forest management by
printing this book on materials made from wood that comes
from responsible sources and reclaimed material

Walther Thun, Beech Tree
near Willingshausen, *1962*
(watercolor, 30 x 56 cm)

When we look more closely at Walter Thun's magical landscapes, we can discern the form of certain beings that he discovered as he was painting and which he made visible in his work. Here he succeeded in expressing in a most wonderful way, the cosmic forces of Saturn, whose influence is so instrumental in giving the beech its typical form and growth pattern.

This quality of Saturn is shown strikingly in the metallic, lead-like radiance of the sunlight that is reflected from the wonderfully glistening siver-grey bark.

Introduction

Looking back at the last two years, we expected very mixed weather in the first part of 2018, but were surprised at the emerging spring and early summer that could hardly have been better for plants and bees. Our bee colony grew a little later, but made more honey than ever. Plants blossomed splendidly, but unfortunately there was an abundance of warmth, not to say heatwaves, that led to a kind of stagnation over summer. The lack of rain in many regions led to droughts and crop damage, especially in areas where irrigation was not possible.

In past years some of the extreme weather conditions could be ameliorated by hoeing or harrowing in the morning or evening. Old gardening wisdom states that hoeing in the evening saves watering, while hoeing in the morning allows excess moisture to evaporate. This is also true for agriculture.

After heavy rainfall hoeing or harrowing in the morning can help plants grow better. This also helps prevent fungal attacks. However, if conditions are too dry, then hoeing or harrowing from the late afternoon onwards can helps. The earth begins to 'breathe in' after this time. Humidity will be better absorbed by the soil, with moisture thus reaching plants.

Judging by the planetary positions, 2020 will be a year dominated by warmth. Jupiter, Saturn and Pluto remain mainly in Sagittarius, leading to a great number of Warmth trines with other planets. Working the soil in the right way can do much to balance these effects. Biodynamic practioners can enhance this by using the appropriate preparations.

Hoeing activates soil organisms, which reconfigure themselves, stimulating plant growth. Every time a garden or field is worked over, nitrogen from the air can enter the soil. This is the simplest and most natural fertilizer we have at our disposal.

Fruit Trees, Vines and Berry Bushes

Matthias Thun

From the early 1950s onwards, Maria Thun sought to research the connection between cosmic events and those occurring on the earth. She gained her initial inspiration from the indications given by Rudolf Steiner in the Agriculture Course. Over the next ten to fifteen years she was able to discover some fundamental principles and then share them with practising farmers. They in turn had further questions which also had to be researched.

This led to a never-ending program of research.

Finding answers to the many new questions that arose through our work was of paramount importance to her. Questions often relate to a specific challenge, such as the leaf blight caused by *Phytophthora infestans*. Or perhaps a gardener has a problem with aphids. In conventional agriculture and horticulture these problems are dealt with using various pesticides. With more and more gardeners opting to go organic and with no recourse to the experiences of earlier generations, it is to us that they frequently turn for advice.

There also appears to be increasing interest in fruit growing. We have therefore decided to devote a major part of this edition of the calendar to the care and cultivation of fruit.

As will become apparent, trees and especially fruit trees share many similarities with annual vegetable crops in terms of their cultivation. This includes vines and soft fruit when it comes to manuring the soil and applying teas.

Our calendar is often mentioned in the same breath as the many Moon calendars. Those who are familiar with the *Maria Thun Biodynamic Calendar*, however, will be aware that the Moon is only one of the influences streaming in from the cosmos. Others include the Sun, the planets and the constellations of the zodiac. In studying the Agriculture Course we find that Rudolf Steiner allocates a great deal of space to the planets. What he says about trees, for instance, is so all-embracing that we can no longer conceive the human being in terms of being simply a farmer, gardener or even a wine grower. Boundaries between the various professions dissolve and each field of activity flows seamlessly into the other.

He describes how a tree should be imagined as 'raised up soil' that extends right out into the branches and that it should be cultivated in just the same way as we would cultivate the soil of a field. The leaves, flowers and fruits can then be imagined as growing out of this 'raised up soil' just as annual plants grow out of the soil on the ground.

If we follow this line of thinking to its logical conclusion, we should be able, via the trunk, to fertilize the herbaceous plants growing in the branches just as we do the vegetables growing in the living soil. The question is then how to treat the trunk in such a way that its substance remains trunk, while at the same time acting as fertile soil for the leaves, flowers and fruit.

In the early days, fruit growers liked to apply tree paste and saw it as a beneficial measure. Many orchardists however were not quite convinced and so applied compost to the trees along the drip line. Farmers started calculating how many kilograms or hundredweight of compost to apply and of course how much was needed to be certain of a good crop. The opinion of those more inclined towards horticulture was that if, for instance, a tree produced 15 baskets of apples, 15 baskets of compost should be applied along the drip line. It was a clever thought, but often proved too much of a good thing and not all trees could cope with it. This showed itself in greater susceptibility to pest and fungal attacks.

Maria Thun tried to look at trees in the way Rudolf Steiner described and after many years of research, the Maria Thun tree paste was created (see p. 11).

Preparation

In the northern hemisphere the fruit orchard year starts at the beginning of November. Well-rotted, earthy compost should be applied (see Composting, p. 10). Once the leaves have fallen, the soil can be cultivated at Fruit times three times in succession, accompanied by a simultaneous application of *barrel preparation* (together with tree paste) on the trunks and branches. This is a variation on previous recommendations for tree paste application.

Spraying of fruit trees

In March, *horn manure preparation* should be applied three times at Fruit times when the soil is being cultivated. Also spray it on the trunks and branches.

When the first leaves appear in spring, a single application of *stinging nettle tea* should be given towards evening. There is often only a limited period to make the first application of stinging nettle tea – with apples, for example, there is a brief window of 2 to 3 days between the buds and leaves opening and the flowers coming out when stinging nettle tea can be sprayed. Stinging nettle tea is of particular value since it gives support to leaf development and renders the upper leaf surface less susceptible to the fungal spores carried by wind and rain.

After blossoming, a first application of *horn silica* can be sprayed on the young leaves. Stirring should take place at a Fruit time and begin half an hour before sunrise. After it has been stirred for an hour it should be sprayed out immediately.

An apple shoot (above, related to Venus). The buds are still small, but the leaves are already so large that an application of stinging nettle tea would be beneficial. This situation only lasts a couple of days and then the flower buds open. The tea application window is therefore very short.

The image on the right shows the flower already going to seed. This is when the spray should be applied.

Early in the morning at Flower times, a spraying of *dandelion flower tea* (to strengthen the silica process in the leaf and ward off potential leaf parasites) and of *camomile tea* (to stimulate calcium processes, invigorate the leaves and render copper treatment unnecessary), can be given.

Yarrow flower tea can be sprayed (separately from horn silica) at Fruit times – this stimulates the potassium process and has the effect of rendering sulphur treatment unnecessary.

It is important that herbal teas are sprayed on the leaves and not the flowers, which are very sensitive and do not respond well to them. In the case of pear, cherry and peach it is likely that the recommended sprays can only be applied once flowering is over. Because the bud and leaf development times of the different varieties are so varied, practitioners will themselves have to determine when to spray.

One tea in particular deserves special mention: *equisetum tea* is often used by organic growers as an all round treatment for fungal diseases and is also applied directly to the soil. It is important to be aware that the effects of equisetum can also be too strong. Time and again trials have shown – and subsequent soil analyses have confirmed – that micro-organisms living in the top inch (2–3 cm) of soil can be negatively affected by equisetum tea.

In the case of peach (above, Venus), sprays are only given once the fruit has formed.

With pears (top right, Venus) it depends on the variety whether stinging nettle tea is sprayed before or after flowering.

For cherries (right, Moon and Mars) it is probably also necessary to wait with spraying until after flowering.

The vine also has a positive response to the spraying of various teas. Depending on variety, the silica preparation can be sprayed for one more time on the mature leaves after harvest. This has a beneficial health effect for the coming year. The tree paste is sprayed once the vines have been pruned. A brush should not be used on the vine.

Fine and healthy potato plants (below) which have been sprayed with stinging nettle tea. Their upper leaf surfaces have been made resistant to the fungal attack that can follow rain and wind.

Good blight control can be achieved by spraying stinging nettle tea on the young potato plants when they are about 4–6 in (10–15 cm) high.

This shows how big the potato needs to be for spraying. At this stage an application of horn silica affects not only leaf development, but also the quality of the tuber.

Like the potato, the tomato also benefits from a tea spray. It is treated with stinging nettle tea and horn silica during the period of its early growth. Treatments with nettle tea and silica spray are only applied to the plants raised in the greenhouse once they have been planted out and after the first new pair of leaves have appeared.

These tomatoes (below right) have been sprayed with oak bark tea and horn silica.

Thoroughly decomposed compost covered with straw.

Harvesting

To support bud formation, horn silica preparation can be applied at Fruit times. The silica should never be applied when the trees are in blossom but only once the fruit has set. Where *summer pruning* is necessary, choose Fruit times during the descending Moon (transplanting times) period.

Choose Flower or Fruit times during the ascending Moon period (that is, not transplanting times) to *harvest fruit* for storing.

A horn silica application can be given *after the harvest* but before leaf fall at Fruit times in the afternoon from 3 pm onwards. This ripens the wood and acts as a preventative against fungal disease in the following year.

This provides a clear plan of action regarding fruit tree management.

Composting

We should also add a word regarding the use of compost. Thoroughly decomposed, earthy compost has been left to mature for a whole year. Throughout this time the compost has absorbed planetary forces. Rudolf Steiner described how everything that is raised above the normal level of the soil becomes specially receptive to cosmic influences.

Such 'cosmic maturity' cannot be achieved by speeding up the process with commercially available organic compost activators. These will bring about rapid biological and chemical changes but not the desired cosmic maturity. The recommended amount of 4–5 tons per acre (10 tonnes/ha) of ripe compost is so small that it is hardly visible and yet it has a very beneficial effect on the life of the soil.

Maria Thun Tree Paste

Finding the right compost and manure

Biodynamic practioners place great store on producing high quality manure and plant composts to improve soil fertility and produce healthy plants. Already in the 1960s as the scope of Maria Thun's research became more extensive, gardeners were asking what type of compost they should use for their various crops. This then led us to begin a whole series of comparative compost trials. Maria Thun could remember from her childhood days how her mother used many different kinds of compost in her kitchen garden. Now however, gardeners needed to produce the appropriate biodynamic compost. So we began to make compost from the manure of cattle, horses, pigs and poultry. Over time these trials gradually became more complex as we found that there was a great deal of variation within each type of manure, depending on where it came from and how it was treated.

Cow manure proved to possess the most balanced of qualities, horse manure always brought warmth and we found pig manure to be only suitable for mixing in with cow or horse manure. The manure from poultry was very specialized and could be used to enrich other forms of compost.

Agriculture was at that time undergoing fundamental changes. Slurry, a mixture of manure and urine, began to dominate the cowsheds and the ancient practice of making hay was gradually being displaced by silage production. The consequence was that the animal manures now had a different effect on the plants and their health. It also affected the production of biodynamic horn manure preparation and altered the way it worked.

Exceptionally well-formed manure.

The manure for making horn manure is dynamized for a whole hour at the cowshed.

The ingredients of tree paste: cowpats, clay, basalt meal, ash and whey.

To make tree paste

Place 22 lb (10 kg) of cowpats in a wooden vessel together with 22 lb clay, 5.5 lb (2.5 kg) basalt meal, 5.5 lb wood ash, 1 quart (1 liter) of whey. Mix it all together with a spade (dynamize it) for a whole hour. The paste can then be kept in a cool dark place and used over a period of several weeks.

For spraying, 1 lb of tree paste should be added to 12 gallons of water (1 kg to 100 liters) and then stirred for twenty minutes with the barrel preparation. It is then allowed to settle before being sieved through two nylon stockings to prevent sprayer nozzles being blocked.

The ingredients are placed in a wooden vessel.

Left: Titia is turning and mixing for one hour (dynamizing).

Below: The finished tree paste.

Friedrich using a wire brush to remove old bark. For younger trees with more delicate bark a bristle brush can be used.

A broad paintbrush is used to apply the tree paste to the bark.

Damaged areas can be treated by applying unthinned tree paste to the affected areas.

A piece of sacking can be tied to the pasted area to prevent it being blown or washed away by rain.

After carrying out many trials we were able to state with some certainty that the manure used for making the preparation should be taken from cows which have been fed roughage (hay and straw) for a few days in order to have firm, well-structured and sweet-smelling manure. We were always pleased to receive manure of this quality from the farmers for our preparations.

Planets and Trees

In the Agriculture Course, Rudolf Steiner referred to the various relationships of trees to the planets. In the first Goetheanum – made entirely out of wood – he created two sets of seven artistically carved planetary pillars: the Moon pillar was made from cherry wood, the Venus pillar from birch wood, the Mercury pillar from elm, the Sun pillar from ash, the Mars pillar from oak, the Jupiter pillar from maple and the Saturn pillar from hornbeam. These are the trees linked to the classical planets.

Planetary rhythms

Let us first of all consider the rhythms of the planets. Saturn takes about 30 years to go around the zodiac. Jupiter's revolution is 12 years, and Mars takes approximately 2 years. The Sun has a median position, taking one year to go around the zodiac, its daily arcs ascending for half the year, and then descending in the other half of the year. Mercury and Venus are always close to the Sun, and on average also take one year to go around the zodiac, but Mercury's revolution around the Sun takes 116 days, and Venus' is 584 days.

The effects are strongest when the planets are in retrograde movement, that is when they are closest to the Earth. The planets' position in the zodiac is also important, as is the relationship of one planet to another – opposition, trine, etc.

Woody plants are dependent on the Sun too, but have an even stronger connection to the planets of our solar system. In the Agriculture Course Rudolf Steiner related the conifers to Saturn and the oak tree to Mars. Later he said: 'Just like the color of flowers, the fine taste of apricots or plums is a cosmic quality that has made its way up into the fruit. In every apple you are actually eating Jupiter, in every plum, Saturn.' On another occasion he brings the life of the tree into connection with the stars.

The fruiting capacity of woody plants is often influenced by the cosmic effect of the planets in the previous year.

Maple *(Acer)* is a Jupiter plant.

The apple tree *(Malus pumila)* is connected to Jupiter.

Birch *(Betula)* belongs to the planet Venus.

Pear *(Pyrus)* is connected to Venus.

Cherry *(Prunus avium)* belongs to the Moon but also partly to Mars.

Beech *(Fagus sylvatica)* reveals the influence of Jupiter and Saturn.

Hornbeam *(Carpinus betulus)* is a Saturn tree.

Oak *(Quercus),* both the common and sessile oak are Mars plants.

Alder *(Alnus glutinosa)* is a Mercury tree.

Ash *(Fraxinus excelsior)* or 'yggdrasil' is linked to the Sun.

Spruce *(Picea abies)* though a conifer, a Saturn plant, is primarily a Sun tree.

Hazel *(Corylus avellana)* is a Sun plant. It is usually referred to as a bush.

Horse chestnut *(Aesculus hippocastanum)* is a Mars plant.

Pine *(Pinus sylvestris)* is as a conifer under the rulership of Saturn and yet at the same time it is a Moon plant.

Larch *(Laris decidua)* is a coniferous tree but has little connection to Saturn. It is more strongly related to the inner planets Venus and Mercury.

The flowers of the lime tree *(Tilia platyphyllos)* and their drowsy scent indicate its connection to Venus.

Sweet chestnut *(Castanea sativa)* expresses the tension between Jupiter and Mars.

The poplar *(Populus)* is a tree that prefers the moist soil of the plain or stream sides. It can be related to the Moon.

Robinia or false acacia *(Robinia pseudoacacia)* is originally from America. It is connected with Venus.

Silver fir *(Abies alba)* is a conifer and hence related to Saturn It also has a strong connection to the Sun.

Thuja occidentalis (arbovitae or norther white-cedar) is a Saturn plant.

English elm *(Ulmus minor)* is connected to Mercury.

Juniper *(Juniperus)* is a Saturn plant.

Walnut *(Juglans regia)* is a Jupiter tree.

Pussy willow or sallow *(Salix caprea)* is grouped among the Venus plants

Cedar of Lebanon *(Cedrus libani)* has a special cultural connection having been used to build the Temple of Solomon. As well as being connected to Saturn, it is also a Sun plant.

The plum *(Prunus domestica)* is a genuine Saturn plant.

Palm trees are monocotyledons, which means having a single seed leaf. The fronds are finely divided. Date and coconut palms are the best known culti-vated plants. Oil from the latter is also used in Europe. They are influenced by several planetary forces. Palms are under the overall influence of Saturn but in their leaves we find the Mercury impulse, in the flowers Venus and in the fruit Jupiter.

Olive *(Olea europaea)*, which belongs to Jupiter, only grows in warm and light-filled regions of the earth. Olive oil is produced from its fruit. It is a valuable and nutritional oil. The yield of oil and its quality can be enhanced if its leaves are sprayed three times with horn silica after flowering early in the morning at Flower times.

Maria Thun's Tree Log Preparations

The biodynamic approach to agriculture involves the use of the preparations recommended by Rudolf Steiner for improving compost and enhancing vitality. Some of these preparations require the use of certain animal organs. With the onset of BSE, access to them became more difficult. This led Maria Thun to investigate whether it would be possible to make preparations without using animal organs. These preparations instead use the bark of trees. They are not counted among the biodynamic preparations developed by Rudolf Steiner. They do, however, build on indications and insights gained through anthroposophy and can be used in biodynamic agriculture.

They are produced in accordance with lunar and planetary rhythms. These need adhering to with some precision otherwise success cannot be guaranteed. The specific times are published in the calendar, but since these constellations do not recur regularly and in some years do not arise at all, it is worth making sufficient preparations to last more than one year, so as to bridge any gap. They should be stored like biodynamic preparations, in pots surrounded by peat.

The Time When the Soil Warms up

For over ten years we have included in our calendar, the date when the soil starts warming up. This concept has frequently caused some consternation and so we thought to address it in more detail.

It came about in connection with the making of the biodynamic compost preparations. We found over many years that the preparations matured at different times, depending on the temperature of the soil. After investigating the times when the preparations were taken out of the earth, we found that the preparations that were retrieved during a particular Mercury constellation were more effective than other similar preparations. Subsequently, in the calendar we always gave a specific day when the soil warmed up. However, we still had the question about whether this was a measurable phenomenon or a conjecture based on intuition.

While I was training to be a beekeeper, the students had to look after the weather station of the bee institute. This also involved measuring the temperature of the soil at a depth of 20 and 40 inches (50 cm and 100 cm). Remembering this we decided to check soil temperatures here in Dexbach. Our house is situated at an altitude of 1200 ft (360 m). Our soils are composed of eroded shale and the bedrock is slate rock.

Using a 3½ inch (9 cm) drill, we drilled a 20 in deep hole and another of 33 in (85 cm) – the deepest that the hard rock allowed. We then inserted the appropriate length of piping into the holes and placed soil thermometers in the holes to measure the temperature. The holes were sited in such a way that they were shaded until the afternoon so that the sun could only influence the temperature later in the day.

We started taking measurements on April 12, 2018. At a depth of 20 inches the temperature was 48°F (9°C) and at 33 in 46°F (8°C). The Mercury constellation that was supposed to warm up the soil was on May 14, 2018. On May 10 the temperatures had already risen slowly to 54°F (12°C) at 20 inches, and 50°F (10°C) at 33 inches depth. During the night from May 13 to 14 at 20 inches it still measured 54°F, but at 33 inches the temperature rose overnight by 4°F (2°C).

That is an enormous rate of increase in such a short time and at such a depth. It also appeared to be connected to the Mercury warmth constellation referred to earlier. It wasn't possible to observe similar temperature differences at 20 in. At that level they were influenced to a greater extent by external temperatures. We intend to continue taking measurements in the coming years in order to reach a more definitive conclusion.

Pipes inserted in the ground into which soil thermometers were placed to measure soil temperatures.

Winter Feed for Bees

The herbal teas recommended as supplements in the feeding of bees prior to winter are all plants that have proved their value over many years. Yarrow, camomile, dandelion and valerian are made by pouring boiling water over the flowers, allowing them to brew for fifteen minutes and then straining them. Stinging nettle, horsetail and oak bark are placed in cold water, brought slowly to the boil and simmered for fifteen minutes. Three grams (1 tablespoon) of each dried herb and half a quart (½ liter) of the prepared teas is enough to produce 25 gal (100 liters) of liquid feed. This is a particularly important treatment in years when there are large amounts of honeydew.

Experiences and considerations

When a beekeeper engages with natural beekeeping he will find himself having to address not only the issue of 'artificial' queen breeding, but also the practice of feeding sugar in the fall.

The widespread view is that the feeding of sugar cannot be avoided. This is particularly true for bees that collect honeydew for there can be problems with overwintering.

In our region, oak and spruce trees produce honeydew and in some years the bees take in huge amounts. Honey flows have been fairly predictable here for many decades. It was seldom possible to take a harvest from the early honey flow. The first harvest of any note generally occurred in mid-June. This was a

Trough hive with honey super on top.

Trough hive before the second harvest. The frames in the space at the rear are well filled with honey and ready for extraction.

very pleasant flower honey made up from the nectar of the orchard and meadow flowers and the first woodland raspberries.

The second harvest came from raspberries, willowherb and the honeydew of oak, spruce and pine. When it was extracted, the color of the honey already indicated that this second harvest would provide a poorer quality winter feed than the richer flower honey that preceded it.

About fifteen years ago there was a restructuring of small farms in our area. The fields under cultivation became fewer, dairy farming declined and the grazing area devoted to fatting bulls and beef suckler herds increased. The organic idea was gradually growing stronger and this resulted in an increase in the amount of nectar available for bees. This meant that the early honey flow from dandelions and fruit orchards became more reliable.

The time had now come for me to rethink my bee management system. The hive I use is the traditional straw skep. In the brood chamber there are 18 frames and in the honey super 10 frames. This size is perfectly adequate for our bees and for this landscape.

We used to install queen excluders between the brood chamber and the honey super in order to have comb for centrifuging that was free of brood. Of the 18 frames in the brood chamber, some 12 to 16 usually contained brood. I have now ceased using queen excluders for a number of years and have found that the brood occupies the front half of both the brood chamber and honey super. The 6 to 8 frames towards the rear are generally free of brood and serve as a honey store.

Matured honey for extracting.

The colonies grow rapidly in springtime thanks to the improvement of the early nectar flow. They bring in a lot of pollen and nectar which is then deposited around the brood in the front portion of what is now a double brood chamber. Once this space has been filled, the remaining honey is stored in the combs towards the rear of the hive. It is the honey from these frames that I harvest in spring.

The brood nest consists of brood surrounded by a good supply of pollen and honey. The honey or nectar that is brought in after the first harvest is put into the empty cells from which the honey has been extracted. Depending on the time of year, this is also where we can find accumulations of honeydew. The honey from these combs is then extracted in the fall and constitutes my second harvest.

During the extraction process care is taken to ensure that the stored honey which largely consists of flower honey from the spring and summer, is retained. For each frame of bees, 2.2 lb (1 kg) of winter feed is needed to enable them to overwinter. The weight of feed can be calculated in the following way: Our frames have an external measurement of 13 x 10 in (33 cm x 25 cm). This is the normal German size. If both sides of the frame are filled with honey it will weigh 4.4 lb (2 kg). This corresponds to an area which can be covered by four hands and is a simple and fairly accurate way to calculate how much stored honey the colonies have.

If additional feeding becomes necessary, the capping honey can be used as a supplement. If necessary, sugar water can also be given at this point.

Here we can clearly see the somewhat viscous honey being extracted from the cells of the comb. There is some dark colored honey on the floor of the centrifuge which does not make good winter feed.

It should be in a ratio of 2:3 which means 1 gal water to 12½ lb sugar (2 liters to 3 kg). One gallon of such a solution provides around 6 lb of winter feed (1 liter provides 750 g). Unfortunately some beekeepers have adopted the habit of continuing to feed the bees with sugar water until they can take no more. That is generally too much and may result in unused sugar appearing in the honey extracted in the spring and thereby reducing its quality.

If the honey upon which the colonies overwinter is not consumed by the time of the first harvest, the old honey can be easily distinguished from the new by the appearance of the cell caps. These will then be left unopened when the honey is extracted.

Some of the late-season honey stored in the vicinity of the brood nest will almost certainly be of honeydew origin. This will, however, be consumed early on and be excreted by the bees during their last flights and present no serious problem in the winter. I might add that for the last four years I have not fed any sugar to our colonies.

There will of course always be sceptics who will find something problematic in what has been described. It confirms for me, however, my experience that beekeeping can be very rewarding even without the highest yields and input of sugar.

The professional beekeeper – I have been a professional beekeeper for about 40 years – will of course find it difficult to accept this approach since he needs to achieve high yields to survive financially.

Background to the Calendar

The zodiac

The **zodiac** is a group of twelve constellations of stars which the Sun, Moon and all the planets pass on their circuits. The Sun's annual path always takes exactly the same line, called **ecliptic.**

The angles between the Sun, Moon and planets are called **aspects.** In this calendar the most important is the 120° angle, or trine.

In the illustration below the outer circle shows the varying sizes of the visible **constellations** of the zodiac. The dates on this outer circle are the days on which the Sun enters the constellation (this can change by one day because of leap years). The inner circle shows the divisions into equal sections of 30° corresponding to the **signs** used in astrology.

It is the *constellations,* not the signs, on which our observations are based, and which are used throughout this calendar.

The twelve constellations are grouped into four different types, each having three constellations at an angle of about 120°, or trine. About every nine days the Moon passes from one type – for instance Root, through the other types (Flower, Leaf and Fruit) – back to the same type again.

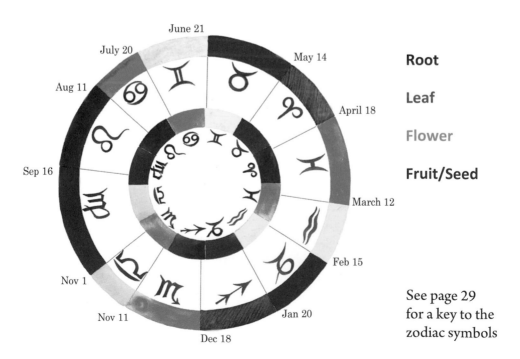

Root

Leaf

Flower

Fruit/Seed

See page 29 for a key to the zodiac symbols

What are oppositions, trines, conjunctions and nodes?

Oppositions ☍

A **geocentric** (Earth-centered) **opposition** occurs when for the observer on the Earth there are two planets opposite one another – 180° apart – in the heavens. They look at one another from opposite sides of the sky and their light interpenetrates. Their rays fall on to the Earth and stimulate in a beneficial way the seeds that are being sown in that moment. In our trials we have found that seeds sown at times of opposition resulted in a higher yield of top quality crops.

At times of opposition two zodiac constellations are also playing their part. If one planet is standing in a Warmth constellation, the second one will usually be in a Light constellation or vice versa. If one planet is in a Water constellation, the other will usually be in an Earth one. (As the constellations are not equally sized, the point opposite may not always be in the opposite constellation.)

With a heliocentric (Sun-centered) opposition an observer would need to place themselves on the Sun. This is of course physically impossible but we can understand it through our thinking. The Sun is in the center and the two planets placed 180° apart also gaze at each other but this time across the Sun. Their rays are also felt by the Earth and stimulate better plant growth. However, heliocentric oppositions are not shown or taken into account in the calendar.

Trines △ or ▲

The twelve constellations are grouped into four different types, each having three constellations at an angle of about 120°, or trine. About every nine days the Moon passes a similar region of forces.

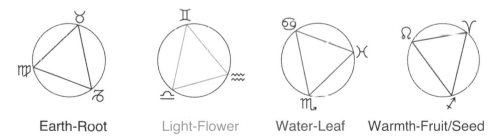

| Earth-Root | Light-Flower | Water-Leaf | Warmth-Fruit/Seed |

Trines occur when planets are 120° from one another. The two planets are then usually both standing in the same elemental configuration – Aries and Leo for example are both Warmth constellations. A Warmth trine means that the effects of these constellations will enhance fruit and seed formation in the plants sown at this time. If two planets are in trine position in Water, watery influences will be enhanced, which usually brings high rainfall. Plants sown at these times will yield more leaf than those at other times. Trine effects can change the way plants grow.

Sometimes when two planets are in a trine, they are in different types of constellations. These are shown as △ under planetary aspects, but have no effect on plant growth and are not shown as colored ▲ in the left-hand pages.

Conjunctions ☌

Conjunctions and multiple conjunctions occur when two or more planets stand behind one another in space. It is then usually only the planet closest to the Earth that has any influence on plant growth. If this influence is stronger than that of the Moon, cosmic disturbances can occur that irritate the plant and cause checks in growth. This negative effect is increased further when the Moon or another planet stands directly in front of another – an occultation (•) or eclipse in the case of Sun and Moon. Sowing at these times will affect subsequent growth detrimentally and harm a plant's regenerative power.

Nodes ☊ and ☋

The Moon's and planets' paths vary slightly, sometimes above and sometimes below the ecliptic. The point at which their paths cross the ecliptic is called a node (☊ is the symbol for ascending node, and ☋ for the descending node). Nodes cause unfavorable times of varying lengths.

If a New Moon is at a node there is a solar eclipse, as the Moon is directly in front of the Sun, while a Full Moon at a node causes a lunar eclipse where the Earth's shadow falls on the Moon. If the Sun or Moon pass exactly in front of a planet, there is an occultation (•). If Mercury or Venus pass exactly in front of the Sun, this is a transit (other planets cannot pass in front of the Sun).

The effects of the Moon

In its 27-day orbit round the Earth, the Moon passes through the constellations of the zodiac and transmits forces to the Earth which affect the four elements: Earth, Light (Air), Water and Warmth (Fire). They in turn affect the four parts of the plant: the roots, the flower, the leaves and the fruit or seeds. The health and growth of a plant can therefore be stimulated by sowing, cultivating and harvesting it in tune with the cycles of the Moon.

These cosmic forces can also be harnessed in beekeeping. By opening and closing the bee 'skep' or box in rhythm with the Moon, the bees' activity is directly affected.

The table below summarizes the effects of the movement of the Moon through the twelve constellations on plants, bees and the weather.

The amount of time the Moon spends in any constellation varies between two and four days. However, this basic framework can be disrupted by planetary oppositions which override the normal tendencies; equally, it may be that trine positions (see pp. 23f) activate a different elemental force to the ones the Moon is transmitting. Times when the Moon's path or a planet's path intersects with the ecliptic (ascending ☊ or descending ☋ node; see page 24) are subject to mainly negative effects. These are intensified if there is an eclipse or occultation, in which case the nearer planet interrupts the influence of the distant one. Such times are unsuitable for sowing or harvesting.

Constellation	Sign	Element		Plant	Bees	Weather
Pisces, Fishes	♓	W	Water	Leaf	Making honey	Damp
Aries, Ram	♈	H	Warmth	Fruit	Gathering nectar	Warm/hot
Taurus, Bull	♉	E	Earth	Root	Building comb	Cool/cold
Gemini, Twins	♊	L	Light	Flower	Gathering pollen	Airy/bright
Cancer, Crab	♋	W	Water	Leaf	Making honey	Damp
Leo, Lion	♌	H	Warmth	Fruit	Gathering nectar	Warm/hot
Virgo, Virgin	♍	E	Earth	Root	Building comb	Cool/cold
Libra, Scales	♎	L	Light	Flower	Gathering pollen	Airy/bright
Scorpio, Scorpion	♏	W	Water	Leaf	Making honey	Damp
Sagittarius, Archer	♐	H	Warmth	Fruit	Gathering nectar	Warm/hot
Capricorn, Goat	♑	E	Earth	Root	Building comb	Cool/cold
Aquarius, Waterman	♒	L	Light	Flower	Gathering pollen	Airy/bright

Good Friday to Easter

Easter is a date set by astronomical events: it is determined by the Full Moon after the spring equinox. Our experience and trials over the last 35 or 40 years have shown that Good Friday and the Saturday are not good times for sowing or transplanting. Seeds sown on those days germinate poorly, plants transplanted on these days don't root properly and most don't survive. This negative effect on plant growth begins in the early morning of Good Friday and ends at sunrise on Easter Sunday, local time. This is why these days are marked as unfavorable in the calendar.

Groupings of plants for sowing and harvesting

When we grow plants, different parts are cultivated for food. We can divide them into four groups.

Root crops at Root times

Radishes, swedes, sugar beet, beetroot, celeriac, carrot, scorzonera, etc., fall into the category of root plants. Potatoes and onions are included in this group too. Root times produce good yields and top storage quality for these crops.

Leaf plants at Leaf times

The cabbage family, lettuce, spinach, lambs lettuce, endive, parsley, leafy herbs and fodder plants are categorized as leaf plants. Leaf times are suitable for sowing and tending these plants but not for harvesting and storage. For this (as well as harvesting of cabbage for sauerkraut) Fruit and Flower times are recommended.

Flower plants at Flower times

These times are favorable for sowing and tending all kinds of flower plants but also for cultivating and spraying 501 (a biodynamic preparation) on oil-bearing plants such as linseed, rape, sunflower, etc. Cut flowers have the strongest scent and remain fresh for longer if cut at Flower times, and the mother plant will provide many new side shoots. If flowers for drying are harvested at Flower times they retain the most vivid colors. If cut at other times they soon lose their color. Oil-bearing plants are best harvested at Flower times.

Fruit Plants at Fruit times

Plants that are cultivated for their fruit or seed belong to this category, including beans, peas, lentils, soya, maize, tomatoes, cucumber, pumpkin, zucchini, but also cereals for summer and winter crops. Sowing oil-bearing plants at Fruit times provides the best yields of seeds. The best time for extraction of oil later on is at Flower times. Leo times are particularly suitable to grow good seed. Fruit plants are best harvested at Fruit times. They store well and their seeds provide good plants for next year. When storing fruit, also remember to choose the time of the ascending Moon.

There is always uncertainty as to which category some plants belong (see list opposite). Onions and beetroot provide a similar yield when sown at Root and Leaf times, but the keeping quality is best from Root times. Kohlrabi and cauliflowers belong to Leaf times, as does Florence fennel (finocchio). Broccoli is more beautiful and firmer when sown at Flower times.

Types of crop

Flower plants

artichoke
broccoli
flower bulbs
flowering ornamental shrubs
flowers
flowery herbs
rose
sunflower

Leaf plants

asparagus
Brussels sprouts
cabbage
cauliflower
celery
chard
chicory (endive)
Chinese cabbage (pe-tsai)
corn salad (lamb's lettuce)
crisphead (iceberg) lettuce
curly kale (green cabbage)
endive (chicory)
finocchio (Florence fennel)
green cabbage (curly kale)
iceberg (crisphead) lettuce
kohlrabi
lamb's lettuce (corn salad)
leaf herbs
leek
lettuce
pe-tsai (Chinese cabbage)
red cabbage
rhubarb
shallots
spinach

Root plants

beetroot
black (Spanish) salsify
carrot
celeriac
garlic
horseradish
Jerusalem artichoke
parsnip
potato
radish
red radish
root tubers
Spanish (black) salsify

Fruit plants

aubergine (eggplant)
bush bean
courgette (zucchini)
cucumber
eggplant (aubergine)
grains
lentil
maize
melon
paprika
pea
pumpkin (squash)
runner bean
soya
squash (pumpkin)
tomato
zucchini (courgette)

Explanations of the Calendar Pages

Next to the date is the constellation in which the Moon is positioned (or constellations, with time of entry into the new one). This is the astronomical constellation, not the astrological sign (see page 22). The next column shows solar and lunar events.

A further column shows which element is dominant on that day (this is also useful for beekeepers). Note H is used for warmth (heat). If there is a change during the day, both elements are mentioned. Warmth effects on thundery days are implied but are not mentioned in this column, but may have a ♄ symbol in the far right 'Weather' column.

The vertical green color band ■ shows Northern Transplanting Time (see next page).

The next column shows in color the part of the plant which will be enhanced by sowing or cultivation on that day. Numbers indicate times of day. On the extreme right, special events in nature are noted as well as anticipated weather changes which disturb or break up the overall weather pattern.

When parts of the plant are indicated that do not correspond to the Moon's position in the zodiac (often it is more than one part on the same day), it is not a misprint, but takes account of other cosmic aspects which overrule the Moon-zodiac pattern and have an effect on a different part of the plant.

Unfavorable times are marked thus ▬. These are caused by eclipses, nodal points of the Moon or the planets or other aspects with a negative influence; they are not elaborated upon in the calendar. If one has to sow at unfavorable times for practical reasons, one can choose favorable times for hoeing, which will improve the plant.

The position of the planets in the zodiac is shown in the box below, with the date of entry into a new constellation. R indicates the planet is moving retrograde (with the date when retrograde begins), D indicates the date when it moves in direct motion again.

On the opposite calendar page astronomical aspects are indicated. Those visible to the naked eye are shown in **bold** type. Visible conjunctions (particularly Mercury's) are not always visible from all parts of the Earth.

Astronomical symbols

Constellations		Planets		Aspects			
♓	Pisces	☉	Sun	☊	Ascending node	**St**	Storms likely
♈	Aries	☾, ☽	Moon	☋	Descending node	♄	Thunder likely
♉	Taurus	☿	Mercury	⌒	Highest Moon	**Eq**	Earthquakes
♊	Gemini	♀	Venus	⌣	Lowest Moon	**Tr**	Traffic dangers
♋	Cancer	♂	Mars	**Pg**	Perigee	**Vo**	Volcanic activity
♌	Leo	♃	Jupiter	**Ag**	Apogee		
♍	Virgo	♄	Saturn	☍	Opposition	▮	Northern Trans-
♎	Libra	♅	Uranus	☌	Conjunction		planting Time
♏	Scorpio	♆	Neptune	☌	Eclipse/occultation		
♐	Sagittarius	♇	Pluto	☍	Lunar eclipse		
♑	Capricorn	○	Full Moon	△	Trine (or ▲)		
♒	Aquarius	●	New Moon	E Earth	L Light/Air W Water H Warmth/Heat		

Transplanting times

From midwinter through to midsummer the Sun rises earlier and sets later each day while its path across the sky ascends higher and higher. From midsummer until midwinter this is reversed, the days get shorter and the midday Sun shines from an ever lower point in the sky. This annual ascending and descending of the Sun creates our seasons. As it ascends and descends during the course of the year, the Sun is slowly moving (from an Earth-centered point of view) through each of the twelve constellations of the zodiac in turn. On average it shines for one month from each constellation.

In the northern hemisphere the winter solstice occurs when the Sun is in the constellation of Sagittarius and the summer solstice when it is in Gemini. At any point from Sagittarius to Gemini the Sun is ascending, while from Gemini to Sagittarius it is descending. In the southern hemisphere this is reversed.

The Moon (and all the planets) follow approximately the same path as the Sun around the zodiac but instead of a year, the Moon takes only about 27½ days to complete one cycle, shining from each constellation in turn for a period of two to three days. This means that the Moon will ascend for about fourteen days and then descend.

It is important to distinguish the journey of the Moon through the zodiac

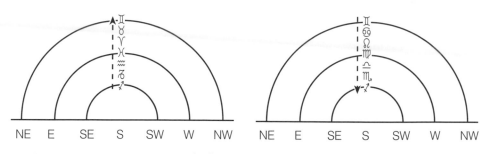

Northern hemisphere ascending Moon (left) and descending Moon (right): Transplanting Time

(siderial rhythm) from the waxing and waning (synodic) cycle: in any given constellation there may be a waxing, waning, full, quarter, sickle or gibbous Moon. As it moves through the zodiac the Moon, like the Sun, is ascending (in the northern hemisphere) when it is in the constellations from Sagittarius to Gemini and descending from Gemini to Sagittarius. In the southern hemisphere it is ascending from Gemini to Sagittarius and descending from Sagittarius to Gemini.

When the Moon is ascending, plant sap rises more strongly. The upper part of the plant fills with sap and vitality. This is a good time for cutting scions (for grafting). Fruit harvested during this period remains fresh for longer when stored.

When the Moon is descending, plants take root readily and connect well with their new location. This period is referred to as the **Transplanting Time.** Moving plants from one location to another is called transplanting. This is the case when young plants are moved from the seedbed into their final growing position but also when the gardener wishes to strengthen the root development of young fruit trees, shrubs or pot plants by frequently re-potting them. Sap movement is slower during the descending Moon. This is why it is a good time for trimming hedges, pruning trees and felling timber as well as applying compost to meadows, pastures and orchards.

Note that sowing is the moment when a seed is put into the soil; either the ascending or descending period can be used. It then needs time to germinate and grow. This is different from *transplanting*, which is best done during the descending Moon. These times are given in the calendar.

Northern Transplanting Times refer to the northern hemisphere, and **Southern Transplanting Times** refer to the southern hemisphere. All other constellations and planetary aspects are equally valid in both hemispheres.

Converting to local time

Times given are Eastern Standard Time (EST), or from March 8 to Oct 31 Eastern Daylight Saving Time (EDT), with ^{a} or $_p$ after the time for am and pm.

Noon is 12_p and midnight is 12^a; the context shows whether midnight at the beginning of the day or at the end is meant; where ambiguous (as for planetary aspects) the time has been adjusted by an hour for clarity.

For different time zones adjust as follows:

Newfoundland Standard Time: add $1\frac{1}{2}^h$
Atlantic Standard Time: add 1^h
Eastern Standard Time: do not adjust
Central Standard Time: subtract 1^h
  For Saskatchewan subtract 1^h, but subtract 2^h from March 8 to Oct 31 (no DST)
Mountain Standard Time: subtract 2^h
  For Arizona subtract 2^h, but subtract 3^h from March 8 to Oct 31 (no DST)
Pacific Standard Time: subtract 3^h
Alaska Standard Time: subtract 4^h
Hawaii Standard Time: subtract 5^h, but subtract 6^h from March 8 to Oct 31 (no DST)

For Central & South America adjust as follows:

Argentina: add 2^h, but add 1^h from March 8 to Oct 31 (no DST)
Brazil (Eastern): Jan 1 to Feb 14 add 3^h; Feb 15 to March 7 add 2^h; March 8 to Oct 31 add 1^h; from Nov 1 add 3^h.
Chile: Jan 1 to March 7 add 2^h; March 8 to April 3 add 1^h; April 4 to Sep 6 do not adjust; Sep 7 to Oct 31 add 1^h; from Nov 1 add 2^h.
Columbia, Peru: do not adjust, but subtract 1^h from March 8 to Oct 31 (no DST).
Mexico (mostly CST): subtract 1^h, but from March 8 to April 3, and from Oct 24 to Oct 31, subtract 2^h

For other countries use *The Maria Thun Biodynamic Calendar* from Floris Books which carries all times in GMT, making it easier to convert to another country's local and daylight saving time.

January 2020

All times in EST

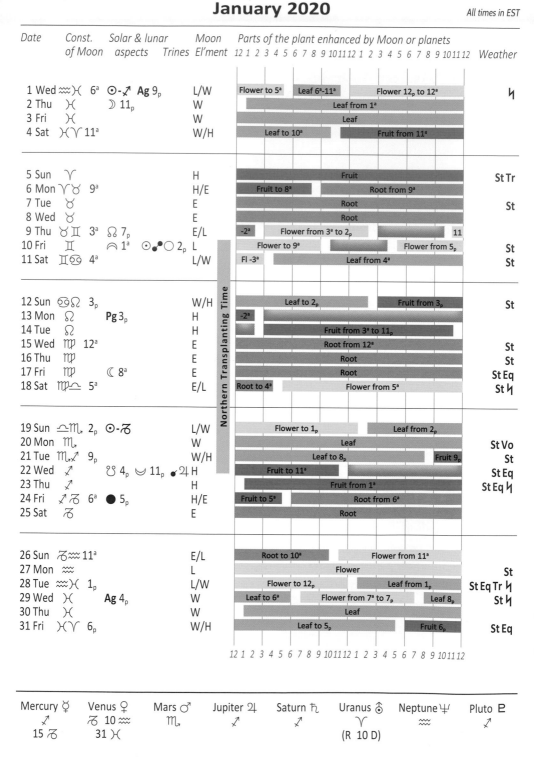

Date	Const. of Moon	Solar & lunar aspects	Trines	Moon El'ment	Parts of the plant enhanced by Moon or planets	Weather
1 Wed ♒︎)(6ᵃ		☉-♐︎ Ag 9ₚ		L/W	Flower to 5ᵃ · Leaf 6ᵃ-11ᵃ · Flower 12ₚ to 12ᵃ	♄
2 Thu)(		☽ 11ₚ		W	Leaf from 1ᵃ	
3 Fri)(				W	Leaf	
4 Sat)(♈︎ 11ᵃ				W/H	Leaf to 10ᵃ · Fruit from 11ᵃ	
5 Sun ♈︎				H	Fruit	St Tr
6 Mon ♈︎♉︎ 9ᵃ				H/E	Fruit to 8ᵃ · Root from 9ᵃ	
7 Tue ♉︎				E	Root	St
8 Wed ♉︎				E	Root	
9 Thu ♉︎♊︎ 3ᵃ		♎ 7ₚ		E/L	-2ᵃ · Flower from 3ᵃ to 2ₚ · 11	
10 Fri ♊︎		☋ 1ᵃ ☉●▪○ 2ₚ		L	Flower to 9ᵃ · Flower from 5ₚ	St
11 Sat ♊︎♋︎ 4ᵃ				L/W	Fl -3ᵃ · Leaf from 4ᵃ	St
12 Sun ♋︎♌︎ 3ₚ				W/H	Leaf to 2ₚ · Fruit from 3ₚ	St
13 Mon ♌︎		Pg 3ₚ		H	-2ᵃ	
14 Tue ♌︎				H	Fruit from 3ᵃ to 11ₚ	
15 Wed ♍︎ 12ᵃ				E	Root from 12ᵃ	St
16 Thu ♍︎				E	Root	St
17 Fri ♍︎		☾ 8ᵃ		E	Root	St Eq
18 Sat ♍︎♎︎ 5ᵃ				E/L	Root to 4ᵃ · Flower from 5ᵃ	St ♄
19 Sun ♎︎♏︎ 2ₚ		☉-♑︎		L/W	Flower to 1ₚ · Leaf from 2ₚ	
20 Mon ♏︎				W	Leaf	St Vo
21 Tue ♏︎♐︎ 9ₚ				W/H	Leaf to 8ₚ · Fruit 9ₚ	St
22 Wed ♐︎		☋ 4ₚ ☌ 11ₚ ▪♃		H	Fruit to 11ᵃ	St Eq
23 Thu ♐︎				H	Fruit from 1ᵃ	St Eq ♄
24 Fri ♐︎♑︎ 6ᵃ		● 5ₚ		H/E	Fruit to 5ᵃ · Root from 6ᵃ	
25 Sat ♑︎				E	Root	
26 Sun ♑︎♒︎ 11ᵃ				E/L	Root to 10ᵃ · Flower from 11ᵃ	
27 Mon ♒︎				L	Flower	St
28 Tue ♒︎)(1ₚ				L/W	Flower to 12ₚ · Leaf from 1ₚ	St Eq Tr ♄
29 Wed)(		Ag 4ₚ		W	Leaf to 6ᵃ · Flower from 7ᵃ to 7ₚ · Leaf 8ₚ	St ♄
30 Thu)(				W	Leaf	
31 Fri)(♈︎ 6ₚ				W/H	Leaf to 5ₚ · Fruit 6ₚ	St Eq

Northern Transplanting Time

Mercury ☿	Venus ♀	Mars ♂	Jupiter ♃	Saturn ♄	Uranus ♅	Neptune ♆	Pluto ♇
♐︎	♑︎ 10 ♒︎	♏︎	♐︎	♐︎	♈︎	♒︎	♐︎
15 ♑︎	31)(				(R 10 D)		

NB: All zodiac symbols refer to astronomical constellations, not astrological signs (see p. 22)

Planetary aspects
(**Bold** = *visible to naked eye*)

January 2020

1	
2	☿☌♃ 12ₚ
3	
4	☽☌☊ 5ₚ
5	
6	
7	☽☍♂ 2ᵃ
8	
9	☽☍♃ 7ₚ
10	☉☌☿ 11ᵃ ☽☍☿ 3ₚ ☽☍♇ 7ₚ ☽☍♄ 7ₚ
11	
12	☿☌♇ 5ᵃ ☿☌♄ 5ᵃ ♄☌♇ 11ᵃ
13	☉☌♇ 8ᵃ ☽☍♀ 9ᵃ ☉☌♄ 10ᵃ
14	☽☍♅ 12ₚ
15	
16	
17	☽☍☊ 6ₚ
18	
19	
20	☽☌♂ 3ₚ
21	
22	☽●♃ 10ₚ
23	
24	☽☌♇ 7ₚ ☽☌♄ 9ₚ
25	☽☌☿ 2ₚ
26	
27	♀☌♅ 3ₚ
28	☽☌♅ 5ᵃ ☽☌♀ 6ᵃ
29	
30	
31	

With Merrcury, Jupiter, Saturn, Uranus and Pluto in the Warmth constellation of Sagittarius, the start of the year is likely to be mild. From the middle of the month, when Mercury moves to Capricorn, it may become a little cooler. Only Mars in Pisces may bring precipitation.

Northern Transplanting Time
Jan 10 3ᵃ to Jan 22 9ₚ
Southern Transplanting Time
Dec 26 to Jan 9 11ₚ and
Jan 23 1ᵃ to Feb 6

The transplanting time is a good time for **pruning fruit trees, vines and hedges.** Fruit and Flower times are preferred for this work. Avoid unfavorable times.

When **milk processing** it is best to avoid unfavorable times. This applies to both butter and cheese making. Milk which has been produced at Warmth/Fruit times yields the highest butterfat content. This is also the case on days with a tendency for thunderstorms. Times of moon perigee (**Pg**) are almost always unfavorable for milk processing and even yoghurt will not turn out well. Starter cultures from such days decay rapidly and it is advisable to produce double the amount the day before. Milk loves Light and Warmth times best of all. Water times are unsuitable.

Planet (naked eye) visibility
Evening: Mercury (from 29th), Venus
All night:
Morning: Mars, Jupiter (from 18th)

Unfavorable time

February 2020

All times in EST

Date	Const. of Moon	Solar & lunar aspects	Trines	Moon El'ment	Parts of the plant enhanced by Moon or planets	Weather

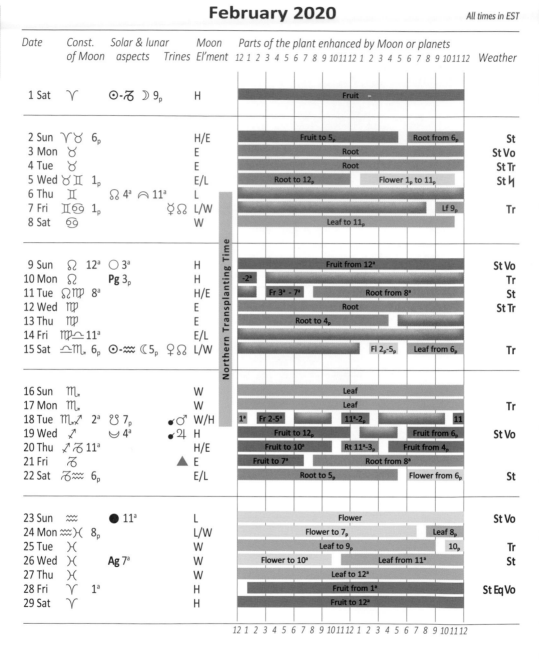

Column scale: 12 1 2 3 4 5 6 7 8 9 10 11 12 1 2 3 4 5 6 7 8 9 10 11 12

Date	Const. of Moon	Solar & lunar aspects	Trines	El'ment	Parts of the plant (bar chart)	Weather
1 Sat	♈	☉-♑ ☽ 9ₚ		H	Fruit	
2 Sun	♈♉ 6ₚ			H/E	Fruit to 5ₚ / Root from 6ₚ	St
3 Mon	♉			E	Root	St Vo
4 Tue	♉			E	Root	St Tr
5 Wed	♉♊ 1ₚ			E/L	Root to 12ₚ / Flower 1ₚ to 11ₚ	St ♄
6 Thu	♊	☍ 4ª ⌢ 11ª		L		
7 Fri	♊♋ 1ₚ		☿☍	L/W	Lf 9ₚ	Tr
8 Sat	♋			W	Leaf to 11ₚ	
9 Sun	♌ 12ª	◯ 3ª		H	Fruit from 12ª	St Vo
10 Mon	♌	Pg 3ₚ		H	-2ª	Tr
11 Tue	♌♍ 8ª			H/E	Fr 3ª - 7ª / Root from 8ª	St
12 Wed	♍			E	Root	St Tr
13 Thu	♍			E	Root to 4ₚ	
14 Fri	♍⌢ 11ª			E/L		
15 Sat	⌢♏ 6ₚ	☉-♒ ☽ 5ₚ ♀☍		L/W	Fl 2ₚ-5ₚ / Leaf from 6ₚ	Tr
16 Sun	♏			W	Leaf	
17 Mon	♏			W	Leaf	Tr
18 Tue	♏♐ 2ª	☍ 7ₚ	•♂	W/H	1ª Fr 2-5ª / 11ª-2ₚ / 11	St Vo
19 Wed	♐	⌣ 4ª	•♃	H	Fruit to 12ₚ / Fruit from 6ₚ	
20 Thu	♐♑ 11ª			H/E	Fruit to 10ª / Rt 11ª-3ₚ / Fruit from 4ₚ	
21 Fri	♑		▲	E	Fruit to 7ª / Root from 8ª	
22 Sat	♑♒ 6ₚ			E/L	Root to 5ₚ / Flower from 6ₚ	St
23 Sun	♒	● 11ª		L	Flower	St Vo
24 Mon	♒♓ 8ₚ			L/W	Flower to 7ₚ / Leaf 8ₚ	
25 Tue	♓			W	Leaf to 9ₚ / 10ₚ	Tr
26 Wed	♓	Ag 7ª		W	Flower to 10ª / Leaf from 11ª	St
27 Thu	♓			W	Leaf to 12ª	
28 Fri	♈ 1ª			H	Fruit from 1ª	St Eq Vo
29 Sat	♈			H	Fruit to 12ª	

Northern Transplanting Time

Column scale: 12 1 2 3 4 5 6 7 8 9 10 11 12 1 2 3 4 5 6 7 8 9 10 11 12

Mercury ☿	Venus ♀	Mars ♂	Jupiter ♃	Saturn ♄	Uranus ♅	Neptune ♆	Pluto ♇
1 ♒	♓	♏	♐	♐	♈	♒	♐
(16 R)		14 ♐					

NB: All zodiac symbols refer to astronomical constellations, not astrological signs (see p. 22)

Planetary aspects
    (**Bold** = *visible to naked eye*)

February 2020

1	☽☌♆ 1ª
2	
3	
4	
5	☽☍♂ 1ª
6	☽☍♃ 4ₚ
7	☽☍♇ 7ª ☿☊ 8ª ☽☍♄ 11ª
8	
9	
10	☾☍☿ 10ª ☾☍♆ 11ₚ
11	
12	☾☍♀ 3ª
13	
14	☾☍♆ 1ª
15	♀☊ 1ª
16	
17	
18	☾☌♂ 8ª
19	☾☌♃ 3ₚ
20	☾☌♇ 3ª ☾☌♄ 9ª
21	♂△♆ 4ª
22	
23	☽☌☿ 8ₚ
24	☽☌♆ 1ₚ
25	☉☌☿ 9ₚ
26	
27	☽☌♀ 12ₚ
28	☽☌♆ 10ª
29	

Jupiter, Saturn, Uranus and Pluto continue in Warmth constellations and are joined by Mars in the middle of the month. This will ensure mild weather. Mercury along with Neptune mediates some Light qualities.

Northern Transplanting Time
Feb 6 1ₚ to Feb 19 2ª
Southern Transplanting Time
Jan 23 to Feb 6 9ª and
Feb 19 6ª to March 4

Vines, fruit trees and shrubs can be pruned during Transplanting Time selecting Flower and Fruit times in preference. Avoid unfavorable times.

Best times for taking **willow cuttings for hedges and fences:** At Flower times outside Transplanting Time. In warm areas at Flower times during Transplanting Time to avoid too strong a sap current.

Planet (naked eye) visibility
Evening: Mercury (to 20th), Venus
All night:
Morning: Mars, Jupiter, Saturn (from 15th)

March

March 2020

All times in EST / EDT

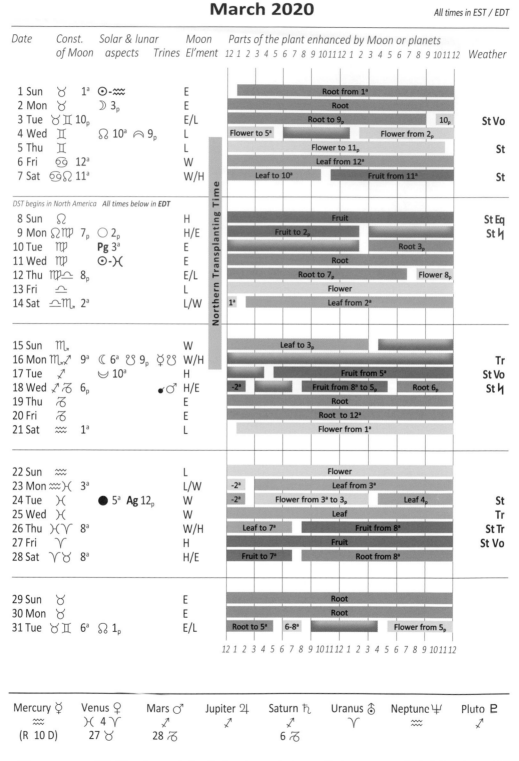

Date	Const. of Moon	Solar & lunar aspects	Trines	Moon El'ment	Parts of the plant enhanced by Moon or planets (12 1 2 3 4 5 6 7 8 9 10 11 12 1 2 3 4 5 6 7 8 9 10 11 12)	Weather
1 Sun	♉ 1^{a}	☉-♒		E	Root from 1^{a}	
2 Mon	♉	☽ 3_{p}		E	Root	
3 Tue	♉♊ 10_{p}			E/L	Root to 9_{p} / 10_{p}	St Vo
4 Wed	♊	☊ 10^{a} ⌒ 9_{p}		L	Flower to 5^{a} / Flower from 2_{p}	
5 Thu	♊			L	Flower to 11_{p}	St
6 Fri	♋ 12^{a}			W	Leaf from 12^{a}	
7 Sat	♋♌ 11^{a}			W/H	Leaf to 10^{a} / Fruit from 11^{a}	St

DST begins in North America *All times below in* ***EDT***

Date	Const. of Moon	Solar & lunar aspects	Trines	Moon El'ment	Parts of the plant enhanced by Moon or planets	Weather
8 Sun	♌			H	Fruit	St Eq
9 Mon	♌♍ 7_{p}	○ 2_{p}		H/E	Fruit to 2_{p}	St ♄
10 Tue	♍	**Pg** 3^{a}		E	Root 3_{p}	
11 Wed	♍	☉-♓		E	Root	
12 Thu	♍♎ 8_{p}			E/L	Root to 7_{p} / Flower 8_{p}	
13 Fri	♎			L	Flower	
14 Sat	♎♏ 2^{a}			L/W	1^{a} / Leaf from 2^{a}	
15 Sun	♏			W	Leaf to 3_{p}	
16 Mon	♏♐ 9^{a}	☾ 6^{a} ☋ 9_{p}	☿☋	W/H		Tr
17 Tue	♐	◡ 10^{a}		H	Fruit from 5^{a}	St Vo
18 Wed	♐♑ 6_{p}		●♂	H/E	-2^{a} / Fruit from 8^{a} to 5_{p} / Root 6_{p}	St ♄
19 Thu	♑			E	Root	
20 Fri	♑			E	Root to 12^{a}	
21 Sat	♒ 1^{a}			L	Flower from 1^{a}	
22 Sun	♒			L	Flower	
23 Mon	♒♓ 3^{a}			L/W	-2^{a} / Leaf from 3^{a}	
24 Tue	♓	● 5^{a} **Ag** 12_{p}		W	-2^{a} / Flower from 3^{a} to 3_{p} / Leaf 4_{p}	St
25 Wed	♓			W	Leaf	Tr
26 Thu	♓♈ 8^{a}			W/H	Leaf to 7^{a} / Fruit from 8^{a}	St Tr
27 Fri	♈			H	Fruit	St Vo
28 Sat	♈♉ 8^{a}			H/E	Fruit to 7^{a} / Root from 8^{a}	
29 Sun	♉			E	Root	
30 Mon	♉			E	Root	
31 Tue	♉♊ 6^{a}	☊ 1_{p}		E/L	Root to 5^{a} / $6\text{-}8^{a}$ / Flower from 5_{p}	

Northern Transplanting Time

12 1 2 3 4 5 6 7 8 9 10 11 12 1 2 3 4 5 6 7 8 9 10 11 12

Mercury ☿	Venus ♀	Mars ♂	Jupiter ♃	Saturn ♄	Uranus ⛢	Neptune ♆	Pluto ♇
♒	♓ 4 ♈	♐	♐	♐	♈	♒	♐
(R 10 D)	27 ♉	28 ♑		6 ♑			

NB: All zodiac symbols refer to astronomical constellations, not astrological signs *(see p. 22)*

Planetary aspects
(**Bold** = *visible to naked eye*)

March 2020

1	
2	
3	
4	☽☌♂ 9ₚ
5	☽☍♃ 12ₚ ☽☍♇ 7ₚ
6	☽☍♄ 1ᵃ
7	

8	☽☍☿ 4ᵃ ☉☌♅ 8ᵃ ♀☌♁ 4ₚ
9	☽☍♆ 12ₚ
10	
11	
12	☾☍♁ 12ₚ ☾☍♀ 7ₚ
13	
14	

15	
16	☿℧ 4ₚ
17	
18	☾☌♂ 5ᵃ ☾☌♃ 7ᵃ ☾☌♇ 11ᵃ ☾☌♄ 9ₚ
19	
20	♂☌♃ 8ᵃ
21	☾☌☿ 5ₚ

22	☾☌♆ 11ₚ
23	♂☌♇ 1ᵃ
24	
25	
26	☽☌♁ 7ₚ
27	
28	♀△♃ 1ᵃ ☽☌♀ 10ᵃ ♀△♇ 11ₚ

29	
30	
31	♂☌♄ 3ₚ

Mercury remains in Aquarius for the whole month, bringing Light, aided by Neptune. The Warmth influence since the beginning of the year, declines a little as Saturn leaves for the cooler constellation of Sagittarius. At the end of the month Venus and Mars join Saturn in Earth constellations bringing some cold.

Northern Transplanting Time
March 4 11ₚ to March 17 8ᵃ
Southern Transplanting Time
Feb 19 to March 4 7ₚ and
March 17 12ₚ to April 1

Willow cuttings for **pollen production** are best cut from March 12 8ₚ to March 14 1ᵃ; and for **honey flow** from March 7 12ₚ to March 9 2ₚ. Avoid unfavorable times.

Cuttings for grafting: Cut outside Transplanting Time during ascending Moon – always choosing times (Fruit, Leaf, etc.) according to the part of plant to be enhanced.

Control slugs: March 6 1ᵃ to March 7 10ᵃ.

Biodynamic preparations
Pick dandelion in March or April in the mornings during Flower times. The flowers should not be quite open in the centre. Dry them on paper in the shade, not in bright sunlight.

Planet (naked eye) visibility
Evening: Venus
All night.
Morning: Mars, Jupiter, Saturn

Unfavorable time

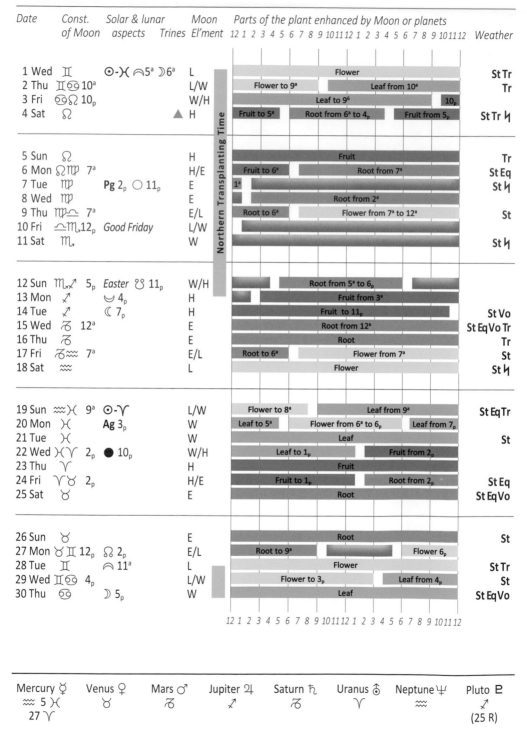

Date	Const. of Moon	Solar & lunar aspects	Trines	Moon El'ment	Parts of the plant enhanced by Moon or planets	Weather
1 Wed	♊	☉-)(⌐5ᵃ ☽6ᵃ		L	Flower	St Tr
2 Thu	♊♋ 10ᵃ			L/W	Flower to 9ᵃ / Leaf from 10ᵃ	Tr
3 Fri	♋♌ 10ₚ			W/H	Leaf to 9ᵍ · 10ₚ	
4 Sat	♌	▲		H	Fruit to 5ᵃ / Root from 6ᵃ to 4ₚ / Fruit from 5ₚ	St Tr ♄
5 Sun	♌			H	Fruit	Tr
6 Mon	♌♍ 7ᵃ			H/E	Fruit to 6ᵃ / Root from 7ᵃ	St Eq
7 Tue	♍	Pg 2ₚ ○ 11ₚ		E	1ᵃ	St ♄
8 Wed	♍			E	Root from 2ᵃ	
9 Thu	♍♎ 7ᵃ			E/L	Root to 6ᵃ / Flower from 7ᵃ to 12ᵃ	St
10 Fri	♎♏ 12ₚ	Good Friday		L/W		St ♄
11 Sat	♏			W		
12 Sun	♏♐ 5ₚ	Easter ☊ 11ₚ		W/H	Root from 5ᵃ to 6ₚ	
13 Mon	♐	☋ 4ₚ		H	Fruit from 3ᵃ	
14 Tue	♐	☾ 7ₚ		H	Fruit to 11ₚ	St Vo
15 Wed	♑ 12ᵃ			E	Root from 12ᵃ	St Eq Vo Tr
16 Thu	♑			E	Root	Tr
17 Fri	♑♒ 7ᵃ			E/L	Root to 6ᵃ / Flower from 7ᵃ	St
18 Sat	♒			L	Flower	St ♄
19 Sun	♒)(9ᵃ	☉-♈		L/W	Flower to 8ᵃ / Leaf from 9ᵃ	St Eq Tr
20 Mon	)(	Ag 3ₚ		W	Leaf to 5ᵃ / Flower from 6ᵃ to 6ₚ / Leaf from 7ₚ	
21 Tue	)(			W	Leaf	St
22 Wed	)(♈ 2ₚ	● 10ₚ		W/H	Leaf to 1ₚ / Fruit from 2ₚ	
23 Thu	♈			H	Fruit	
24 Fri	♈♉ 2ₚ			H/E	Fruit to 1ₚ / Root from 2ₚ	St Eq
25 Sat	♉			E	Root	St Eq Vo
26 Sun	♉			E	Root	St
27 Mon	♉♊ 12ₚ	♌ 2ₚ		E/L	Root to 9ᵃ / Flower 6ₚ	St Tr
28 Tue	♊	⌐ 11ᵃ		L	Flower	St
29 Wed	♊♋ 4ₚ			L/W	Flower to 3ₚ / Leaf from 4ₚ	St
30 Thu	♋	☽ 5ₚ		W	Leaf	St Eq Vo

Northern Transplanting Time

12 1 2 3 4 5 6 7 8 9 10 11 12 1 2 3 4 5 6 7 8 9 10 11 12

Mercury ☿	Venus ♀	Mars ♂	Jupiter ♃	Saturn ♄	Uranus ⛢	Neptune ♆	Pluto ♇
♒ 5)(	♉	♑	♐	♑	♈	♒	♐
27 ♈							(25 R)

NB: All zodiac symbols refer to astronomical constellations, not astrological signs (see p. 22)

Planetary aspects
(**Bold** = *visible to naked eye*)

April 2020

Day	Aspects
1	
2	☽♂♃ 5ᵃ ☽♂♇ 5ᵃ ☽♂♄ 4ₚ ☽♂♂ 6ₚ
3	☿♂♆ 9ₚ
4	♀△♄ 1ₚ ♃♂♇ 10ₚ
5	
6	☽♂♆ 1ᵃ ☽♂☿ 6ᵃ
7	
8	
9	☾♂⊕ 1ᵃ
10	
11	☾♂♀ 3ᵃ
12	
13	
14	☾♂♇ 6ₚ ☾♂♃ 8ₚ
15	☾♂♄ 6ᵃ
16	☾☌♂ 2ᵃ
17	
18	
19	☾♂♆ 7ᵃ
20	
21	☾♂☿ 4ₚ
22	
23	☽♂⊕ 5ᵃ
24	
25	
26	☉♂⊕ 5ᵃ ☽♂♀ 1ₚ
27	
28	
29	☽♂♇ 12ₚ ☽♂♃ 4ₚ
30	☽♂♄ 1ᵃ

Venus, Mars and Saturn in Earth constellations bring cold, but they are balanced by Jupiter, Uranus and Pluto in Warmth constellations. When Mercury enters Pisces on March 5 we can expect some rainy days.

Northern Transplanting Time
April 1 7ᵃ to April 13 2ₚ and
April 28 1ₚ to May 10
Southern Transplanting Time
March 17 to April 1 3ᵃ and
April 13 6ₚ to April 28 9ᵃ

The **soil warms up** on April 27.

Grafting of fruiting shrubs at Fruit times outside transplanting times.
Grafting of flowering shrubs at Flower times outside transplanting times.

Control
Slugs from April 2 10ᵃ to April 3 9ₚ.
Clothes and wax moths from April 19 9ᵃ to April 22 1ₚ

Biodynamic preparations
Maria Thun's tree log preparations: Cut birch, fill with yarrow and hang on April 4, 10ᵃ to 12ₚ.

Planet (naked eye) visibility
Evening: Venus
All night:
Morning: Mars, Jupiter, Saturn

■ *Unfavorable time*

May 2020

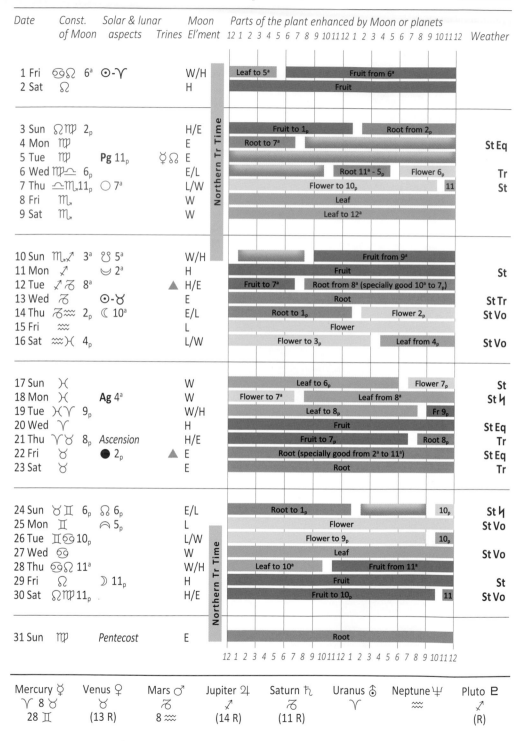

Date	Const. of Moon	Solar & lunar aspects	Trines	Moon El'ment	Parts of the plant enhanced by Moon or planets	Weather
1 Fri	♋♌ 6ᵃ	☉-♈		W/H	Leaf to 5ᵃ / Fruit from 6ᵃ	
2 Sat	♌			H	Fruit	
3 Sun	♌♍ 2ₚ			H/E	Fruit to 1ₚ / Root from 2ₚ	
4 Mon	♍			E	Root to 7ᵃ	St Eq
5 Tue	♍	Pg 11ₚ	☿♌	E		Tr
6 Wed	♍♎ 6ₚ			E/L	Root 11ᵃ - 5ₚ / Flower 6ₚ	St
7 Thu	♎♏ 11ₚ	○ 7ᵃ		L/W	Flower to 10ₚ 11	
8 Fri	♏			W	Leaf	
9 Sat	♏			W	Leaf to 12ᵃ	
10 Sun	♏♐ 3ᵃ	☊ 5ᵃ		W/H	Fruit from 9ᵃ	
11 Mon	♐	☋ 2ᵃ		H	Fruit	St
12 Tue	♐♑ 8ᵃ		▲	H/E	Fruit to 7ᵃ / Root from 8ᵃ (specially good 10ᵃ to 7ₚ)	St Tr
13 Wed	♑	☉-♉		E	Root	St Vo
14 Thu	♑♒ 2ₚ	☽ 10ᵃ		E/L	Root to 1ₚ / Flower 2ₚ	St Vo
15 Fri	♒			L	Flower	
16 Sat	♒♓ 4ₚ			L/W	Flower to 3ₚ / Leaf from 4ₚ	St Vo
17 Sun	♓			W	Leaf to 6ₚ / Flower 7ₚ	St
18 Mon	♓	Ag 4ᵃ		W	Flower to 7ᵃ / Leaf from 8ᵃ	St ♄
19 Tue	♓♈ 9ₚ			W/H	Leaf to 8ₚ / Fr 9ₚ	
20 Wed	♈			H	Fruit	St Eq
21 Thu	♈♉ 8ₚ	Ascension		H/E	Fruit to 7ₚ / Root 8ₚ	Tr
22 Fri	♉	● 2ₚ	▲	E	Root (specially good from 2ᵃ to 11ᵃ)	St Eq
23 Sat	♉			E	Root	Tr
24 Sun	♉♊ 6ₚ	♌ 6ₚ		E/L	Root to 1ₚ 10ₚ	St ♄
25 Mon	♊	♋ 5ₚ		L	Flower	St Vo
26 Tue	♊♋ 10ₚ			L/W	Flower to 9ₚ 10ₚ	
27 Wed	♋			W	Leaf	St Vo
28 Thu	♋♌ 11ᵃ			W/H	Leaf to 10ᵃ / Fruit from 11ᵃ	
29 Fri	♌	☽ 11ₚ		H	Fruit	St
30 Sat	♌♍ 11ₚ			H/E	Fruit to 10ₚ 11	St Vo
31 Sun	♍	Pentecost		E	Root	

Northern Tr Time

12 1 2 3 4 5 6 7 8 9 10 11 12 1 2 3 4 5 6 7 8 9 10 11 12

Mercury ☿	Venus ♀	Mars ♂	Jupiter ♃	Saturn ♄	Uranus ⛢	Neptune ♆	Pluto ♇
♈ 8 ♉	♉	♑	♐	♑	♈	♒	♐
28 ♊	(13 R)	8 ♒	(14 R)	(11 R)			(R)

NB: All zodiac symbols refer to astronomical constellations, not astrological signs (see p. 22)

Planetary aspects
(**Bold** = *visible to naked eye*)

May 2020

May continues in the tension between Earth constellations with Mercury, Venus and Saturn, and Warmth constellations with Jupiter, Uranus and Pluto. Neptune and in the second week Mars bring Light influences.

Northern Transplanting Time
April 28 to May 10 11$_p$ and
May 25 7$_p$ to June 7
Southern Transplanting Time
May 11 4^a to May 25 3$_p$

Transplant **table potatoes** at Root times.
Transplant **seed potatoes** for 2021 from May 19 9$_p$ to May 21 7$_p$.

Hay should be cut between May 24 10$_p$ and May 26 9$_p$, and at other Flower times.

Control:
Moths from May 16 4$_p$ to May 19 8$_p$.
Flies by burning fly papers in the cow barn at Flower times.
Mole crickets ash from May 7 11$_p$ to May 10 2^a.

Begin **queen bee** rearing (grafting or larval transfer, comb insertion, cell punching) between May 24 10$_p$ and May 26 9$_p$ and at other Flower times.

Biodynamic preparations
The preparations can be taken out of the ground after May 7 avoiding unfavourable times (best at Fruit or Flower times). Preparations put into the ground after Sep 15, 2019, should wait to the end of May.

Day	Aspects
1	☿☌⊕ 1^a ☽☍♂ 12$_p$
2	
3	☽☍♆ 11^a
4	☉☌☿ 6$_p$
5	☿♌ 8^a
6	☽☍⊕ 3$_p$
7	☾☍☿ 1$_p$
8	
9	☿△♇ 9^a ☾☍♀ 3$_p$
10	☿△♃ 11^a
11	
12	☾☌♇ 2^a ☾☌♃ 7^a ☾☌♄ 3$_p$ ☿△♄ 4$_p$
13	
14	
15	☾☌♂ 1^a ☉△♇ 3^a
16	☾☌♆ 3$_p$
17	☉△♃ 1$_p$
18	
19	
20	☾☌⊕ 2$_p$
21	
22	☿☌♀ 5^a ☉△♄ 8^a
23	☽☌♀ 11$_p$
24	☽☌☿ 7^a
25	
26	☽☍♇ 5$_p$ ☽☍♃ 9$_p$
27	☽☍♄ 6^a
28	
29	
30	☽☍♂ 4^a ☽☍♆ 7$_p$
31	

Planet (naked eye) visibility
Evening: Mercury (from 15th), Venus (to 29th)
All night: Mars
Morning: Jupiter, Saturn

Unfavorable time

June 2020

Date	Const. of Moon	Solar & lunar aspects	Trines	Moon El'ment	Parts of the plant enhanced by Moon or planets	Weather

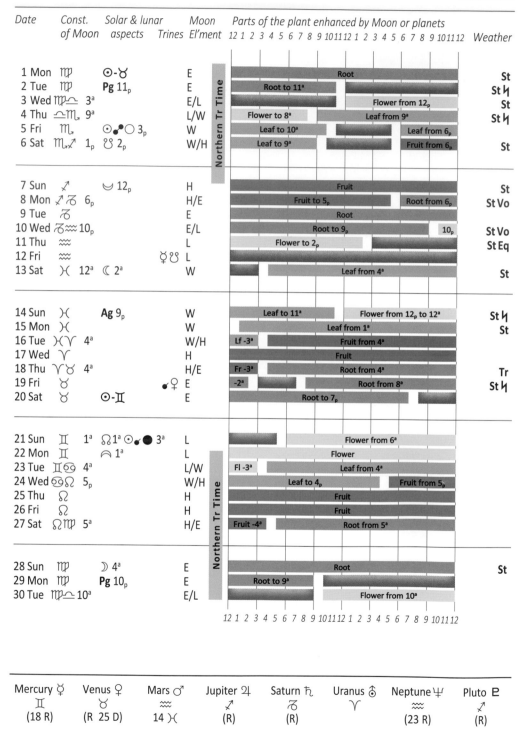

Plant-enhancement chart, left column "Northern Tr Time":

- 1 Mon ♍ ⊙-♉ — E — Root — St
- 2 Tue ♍ Pg 11ₚ — E — Root to 11ᵃ — St ♄
- 3 Wed ♍♎ 3ᵃ — E/L — Flower from 12ₚ — St
- 4 Thu ♎♏ 9ᵃ — L/W — Flower to 8ᵃ / Leaf from 9ᵃ — St ♄
- 5 Fri ♏ ⊙•☌○ 3ₚ — W — Leaf to 10ᵃ / Leaf from 6ₚ —
- 6 Sat ♏♐ 1ₚ ☋ 2ₚ — W/H — Leaf to 9ᵃ / Fruit from 6ₚ — St

- 7 Sun ♐ ☽ 12ₚ — H — Fruit — St
- 8 Mon ♐♑ 6ₚ — H/E — Fruit to 5ₚ / Root from 6ₚ — St Vo
- 9 Tue ♑ — E — Root —
- 10 Wed ♑♒ 10ₚ — E/L — Root to 9ₚ / 10ₚ — St Vo
- 11 Thu ♒ — L — Flower to 2ₚ — St Eq
- 12 Fri ♒ ☿☋ — L — —
- 13 Sat ♓ 12ᵃ ☾ 2ᵃ — W — Leaf from 4ᵃ — St

- 14 Sun ♓ Ag 9ₚ — W — Leaf to 11ᵃ / Flower from 12ₚ to 12ᵃ — St ♄
- 15 Mon ♓ — W — Leaf from 1ᵃ — St
- 16 Tue ♓♈ 4ᵃ — W/H — Lf -3ᵃ / Fruit from 4ᵃ —
- 17 Wed ♈ — H — Fruit —
- 18 Thu ♈♉ 4ᵃ — H/E — Fr -3ᵃ / Root from 4ᵃ — Tr
- 19 Fri ♉ •♀ — E — -2ᵃ / Root from 8ᵃ — St ♄
- 20 Sat ♉ ⊙-♊ — E — Root to 7ₚ —

- 21 Sun ♊ 1ᵃ ☋1ᵃ ⊙•● 3ᵃ — L — Flower from 6ᵃ —
- 22 Mon ♊ ☋ 1ᵃ — L — Flower —
- 23 Tue ♊♋ 4ᵃ — L/W — Fl -3ᵃ / Leaf from 4ᵃ —
- 24 Wed ♋♌ 5ₚ — W/H — Leaf to 4ₚ / Fruit from 5ₚ —
- 25 Thu ♌ — H — Fruit —
- 26 Fri ♌ — H — Fruit —
- 27 Sat ♌♍ 5ᵃ — H/E — Fruit -4ᵃ / Root from 5ᵃ —

- 28 Sun ♍ ☽ 4ᵃ — E — Root — St
- 29 Mon ♍ Pg 10ₚ — E — Root to 9ᵃ —
- 30 Tue ♍♎ 10ᵃ — E/L — Flower from 10ᵃ —

Mercury ☿	Venus ♀	Mars ♂	Jupiter ♃	Saturn ♄	Uranus ♅	Neptune ♆	Pluto ♇
♊	♉	♒	♐	♑	♈	♒	♐
(18 R)	(R 25 D)	14 ♓	(R)	(R)		(23 R)	(R)

NB: All zodiac symbols refer to astronomical constellations, not astrological signs (see p. 22)

Planetary aspects
(**Bold** = *visible to naked eye*)

1	
2	
3	☽☍⚷ 2^a ☉☌♀ 2_p
4	
5	☽☍♀ 10^a
6	
7	**☾☍☿ 10^a**
8	**☾☌♇ 11^a ☾☌♃ 2_p ☾☌♄ 11_p**
9	
10	
11	
12	☿☍ 3_p **☾☌♂ 10_p ☾☌♆ 11_p**
13	♂☌♆ 10^a
14	
15	
16	
17	**☾☌⚷ 1^a**
18	
19	**☾●♀ 5^a**
20	
21	
22	☽☌☿ 4^a ☽☍♇ 10_p
23	☽☍♃ 1^a ☽☍♄ 10^a
24	
25	
26	
27	☽☍♆ 1^a ☽☍♂ 4_p
28	
29	
30	♃☌♇ 2^a ☽☍⚷ 11^a ☉☌☿ 11_p

Planet (naked eye) visibility
Evening: Mercury (to 12th)
All night: Mars, Jupiter, Saturn
Morning: Venus (from 16th)

June 2020

There is a mixed picture for June. There are Warmth, Light and Earth constellations. Jupiter and Pluto in Sagittarius and Uranus in Aries are in Warmth constellations, while Mercury and Neptune are in Light constellations, intensifying the effect in their retrograde motion in the second half of the month. Venus in Taurus and Saturn in Capricorn are also retrograde strengthening the cold effect of the Earth constellations. Mars in the second half of the momth moves into Watery Pisces.

Northern Transplanting Time
May 25 to June 7 10^a and
June 22 2^a to July 4
Southern Transplanting Time
June 7 2_p to June 21 10_p

Cut **hay** at Flower times.

Begin **queen bee** rearing at Fruit and Flower times, avoiding unfavorable times.

Control:
Chitinous insects, wheat weevil, Colorado beetle and varroa from June 18 4^a to June 20 11_p.
Flies by burning fly papers in the cow barn from June 3 3^a to June 4 8^a, and at other Flower times.
Grasshoppers from June 10 10_p to June 12 11_p.

■ *Unfavorable time*

JUNE

July 2020

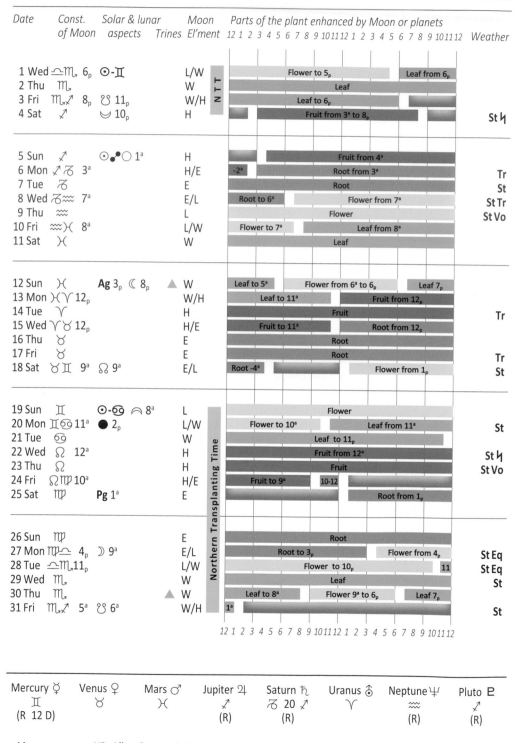

Date	Const. of Moon	Solar & lunar aspects	Trines	Moon El'ment	Parts of the plant enhanced by Moon or planets	Weather
1 Wed	♎︎♏︎ 6ₚ	☉-♊︎		L/W	Flower to 5ₚ Leaf from 6ₚ	
2 Thu	♏︎			W	Leaf	
3 Fri	♏︎♐︎ 8ₚ	☋ 11ₚ		W/H	Leaf to 6ₚ	
4 Sat	♐︎	☽ 10ₚ		H	Fruit from 3ᵃ to 8ₚ	St ♄
5 Sun	♐︎	☉ ● ○ 1ᵃ		H	Fruit from 4ᵃ	
6 Mon	♐︎♑︎ 3ᵃ			H/E	-2ᵃ Root from 3ᵃ	Tr
7 Tue	♑︎			E	Root	St
8 Wed	♑︎♒︎ 7ᵃ			E/L	Root to 6ᵃ Flower from 7ᵃ	St Tr
9 Thu	♒︎			L	Flower	St Vo
10 Fri	♒︎♓︎ 8ᵃ			L/W	Flower to 7ᵃ Leaf from 8ᵃ	
11 Sat	♓︎			W	Leaf	
12 Sun	♓︎	Ag 3ₚ ☾ 8ₚ	▲	W	Leaf to 5ᵃ Flower from 6ᵃ to 6ₚ Leaf 7ₚ	
13 Mon	♓︎♈︎ 12ₚ			W/H	Leaf to 11ᵃ Fruit from 12ₚ	
14 Tue	♈︎			H	Fruit	Tr
15 Wed	♈︎♉︎ 12ₚ			H/E	Fruit to 11ᵃ Root from 12ₚ	
16 Thu	♉︎			E	Root	
17 Fri	♉︎			E	Root	Tr
18 Sat	♉︎♊︎ 9ᵃ	☋ 9ᵃ		E/L	Root -4ᵃ Flower from 1ₚ	St
19 Sun	♊︎	☉-♋︎ ⌒ 8ᵃ		L	Flower	
20 Mon	♊︎♋︎ 11ᵃ	● 2ₚ		L/W	Flower to 10ᵃ Leaf from 11ᵃ	St
21 Tue	♋︎			W	Leaf to 11ₚ	
22 Wed	♋︎ 12ᵃ			H	Fruit from 12ᵃ	St ♄
23 Thu	♋︎			H	Fruit	St Vo
24 Fri	♋︎♍︎ 10ᵃ			H/E	Fruit to 9ᵃ 10-12 Root from 1ₚ	
25 Sat	♍︎	Pg 1ᵃ		E		
26 Sun	♍︎			E	Root	
27 Mon	♍︎♎︎ 4ₚ	☽ 9ᵃ		E/L	Root to 3ₚ Flower from 4ₚ	St Eq
28 Tue	♎︎♏︎ 11ₚ			L/W	Flower to 10ₚ 11	St Eq
29 Wed	♏︎			W	Leaf	St
30 Thu	♏︎		▲	W	Leaf to 8ᵃ Flower 9ᵃ to 6ₚ Leaf 7ₚ	
31 Fri	♏︎♐︎ 5ᵃ	☋ 6ᵃ		W/H	1ᵃ	St

Northern Transplanting Time

Mercury ☿	Venus ♀	Mars ♂	Jupiter ♃	Saturn ♄	Uranus ⛢	Neptune ♆	Pluto ♇
♊︎	♉︎	♓︎	♐︎	♑︎ 20 ♐︎	♈︎	♒︎	♐︎
(R 12 D)			(R)	(R)		(R)	(R)

NB: All zodiac symbols refer to astronomical constellations, not astrological signs (see p. 22)

Planetary aspects
*(**Bold** = visible to naked eye)*

1
2 ☽♂°♀ 8ᵃ
3
4 ☽♂°☿ 2ₚ

5 **☾☌♃ 6ₚ** **☾☌♇ 7ₚ**
6 **☾☌♄ 6ᵃ**
7
8
9
10 **☾☌♅ 7ᵃ**
11 **☾☌♂ 5ₚ**

12 ☉△♆ 3ₚ
13
14 ☉♂°⚷ 4ᵃ **☾☌♁ 10ᵃ**
15 ☉♂°♇ 3ₚ
16
17 **☾☌♀ 3ᵃ**
18

19 **☾☌☿ 1ᵃ**
20 **☾♂°⚷ 1ᵃ** **☾♂°♇ 5ᵃ** ☽♂°♄ 2ᵤ ☉♂°♄ 6ₚ
21
22
23
24 ☽♂°♆ 6ᵃ
25

26 ☽♂°♂ 1ᵃ
27 ☽♂°♁ 6ₚ
28
29
30 ☿☌♃ 10ᵃ ☿△♆ 3ₚ ☽♂°♀ 8ₚ
31

Planet (naked eye) visibility
Evening:
All night: Mars, Jupiter, Saturn
Morning: Mercury (from 22nd), Venus

July 2020

Venus and Saturn (until July 20) are in Earth constellations. Their cold influence will be balanced by Jupiter, Uranus and Pluto in Warmth constellations. The two Light trines are supported by Mercury and Neptune in Gemini and Aquarius. only Mars is in a Water constellation hopefully bringing some rain.

Northern Transplanting Time
June 22 to July 4 8ₚ and
July 19 10ᵃ to Aug 1
Southern Transplanting Time
July 5 1ᵃ to July 19 6ᵃ

Late hay cut at Flower times.

Summer harvest for seeds.
Flower plants: Harvest at Flower times, specially in the first half of the month.
  Fruit plants from July 22 1ᵃ to July 24 9ᵃ, or at other Fruit times.
  Harvest **leaf plants** at Leaf times.
  Harvest **root plants** at Root times, especially July 15 12ₚ to July 18 4ᵃ, and July 25 1ₚ to July 27 3ₚ.
  Always avoid unfavorable times.

Control
Flies: burn fly papers in the cow barn at Flower times.
Slugs: burn from July 20 11ᵃ to July 21 11ₚ. Spray leaf plants and the soil with horn silica early in the morning during Leaf times.
Grasshoppers from July 8 7ᵃ to July 10 7ᵃ.

Biodynamic preparations
Maria Thun's tree log preparations: Cut **larch** and fill with camomile and put it in the ground on July 30 between 8ᵃ and 4ₚ.

July

Date	Const. of Moon	Solar & lunar aspects	Moon Trines	El'ment	Parts of the plant enhanced by Moon or planets 12 1 2 3 4 5 6 7 8 9 10 11 12 1 2 3 4 5 6 7 8 9 10 11 12	Weather

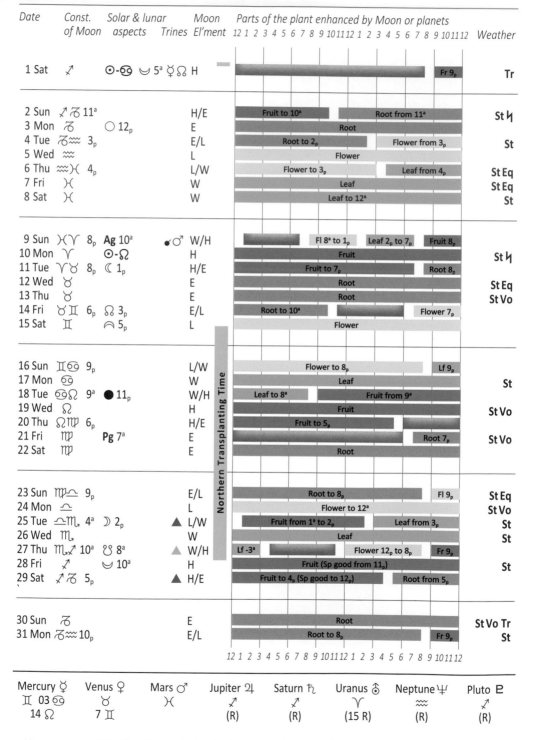

Date	Const.	Aspects	Trines	El'ment	Plant parts	Weather
1 Sat	♐	☉-♋ ☽ 5ᵃ ☿ ☊		H	Fr 9ₚ	Tr
2 Sun	♐♑ 11ᵃ			H/E	Fruit to 10ᵃ Root from 11ᵃ	St ♄
3 Mon	♑	○ 12ₚ		E	Root	
4 Tue	♑♒ 3ₚ			E/L	Root to 2ₚ Flower from 3ₚ	St
5 Wed	♒			L	Flower	
6 Thu	♒♓ 4ₚ			L/W	Flower to 3ₚ Leaf from 4ₚ	St Eq
7 Fri	♓			W	Leaf	St Eq
8 Sat	♓			W	Leaf to 12ᵃ	St
9 Sun	♓♈ 8ₚ	**Ag** 10ᵃ	☌♂	W/H	Fl 8ᵃ to 1ₚ Leaf 2ₚ to 7ₚ Fruit 8ₚ	
10 Mon	♈	☉-♌		H	Fruit	St ♄
11 Tue	♈♉ 8ₚ	☾ 1ₚ		H/E	Fruit to 7ₚ Root 8ₚ	
12 Wed	♉			E	Root	St Eq
13 Thu	♉			E	Root	St Vo
14 Fri	♉♊ 6ₚ	☊ 3ₚ		E/L	Root to 10ᵃ Flower 7ₚ	
15 Sat	♊	⌒ 5ₚ		L	Flower	
16 Sun	♊♋ 9ₚ			L/W	Flower to 8ₚ Lf 9ₚ	
17 Mon	♋			W	Leaf	St
18 Tue	♋♌ 9ᵃ	● 11ₚ		W/H	Leaf to 8ᵃ Fruit from 9ᵃ	
19 Wed	♌			H	Fruit	St Vo
20 Thu	♌♍ 6ₚ			H/E	Fruit to 5ₚ	St Vo
21 Fri	♍	**Pg** 7ᵃ		E	Root 7ₚ	St Vo
22 Sat	♍			E	Root	
23 Sun	♍♎ 9ₚ			E/L	Root to 8ₚ Fl 9ₚ	St Eq
24 Mon	♎			L	Flower to 12ᵃ	St Vo
25 Tue	♎♏ 4ᵃ	☽ 2ₚ	▲	L/W	Fruit from 1ᵃ to 2ₚ Leaf from 3ₚ	St
26 Wed	♏			W	Leaf	St
27 Thu	♏♐ 10ᵃ	☍ 8ᵃ	▲	W/H	Lf -3ᵃ Flower 12ₚ to 8ₚ Fr 9ₚ	
28 Fri	♐	☽ 10ᵃ		H	Fruit (Sp good from 11ₚ)	St
29 Sat	♐♑ 5ₚ		▲	H/E	Fruit to 4ₚ (Sp good to 12ₚ) Root from 5ₚ	
30 Sun	♑			E	Root	St Vo Tr
31 Mon	♑♒ 10ₚ			E/L	Root to 8ₚ Fr 9ₚ	St

Northern Transplanting Time

12 1 2 3 4 5 6 7 8 9 10 11 12 1 2 3 4 5 6 7 8 9 10 11 12

Mercury ☿	Venus ♀	Mars ♂	Jupiter ♃	Saturn ♄	Uranus ⛢	Neptune ♆	Pluto ♇
♊ 03 ♋	♉	♓	♐	♐	♈	♒	♐
14 ♌	7 ♊		(R)	(R)	(15 R)	(R)	(R)

NB: All zodiac symbols refer to astronomical constellations, not astrological signs (see p. 22)

1 ☿☍♇ 7ᵃ ☿☊ 8ᵃ ☽☌♃ 8ₚ

2 ☽☍♇ 3ᵃ ☽☌♄ 10ᵃ ☽☍☿ 11ᵃ
3 ☿☍♄ 5ₚ
4
5
6 ☾☌♆ 2ₚ
7
8

9 ☾●♂ 5ᵃ
10 ☾☌⊕ 7ₚ
11
12
13
14
15 ☾☌♀ 9ᵃ

16 ☾☍♃ 6ᵃ ☉△♂ 10ᵃ ☾☍♇ 1ₚ ☾☍♄ 8ₚ
17 ☿△♂ 2ᵃ ☉☌☿ 11ᵃ
18
19 ☽☌☿ 2ᵃ
20 ☽☍♆ 1ₚ
21
22

23 ☽☍♂ 1ᵃ
24 ☽☍⊕ 1ᵃ
25 ☿△⊕ 11ᵃ ♀☌☊♃ 6ₚ
26
27 ♀△♆ 5ₚ
28 ☽☌♃ 10ₚ
29 ☽☍♀ 5ᵃ ☽☍♇ /ᵃ ☿△♃ 9ᵃ ☽☌♄ 1ₚ

30 ♀☍♇ 9ᵃ ☿☍♆ 3ₚ
31

Planet (naked eye) visibility
Evening:
All night: Mars, Jupiter, Saturn
Morning: Mercury (to 7th), Venus

August is dominated by Warmth constellations, reinforced by two Warmth trines at the end of the month. To begin with, however, Venus is in an Earth, after a week moving to a Light constellation where together with Uranus they make a Light Trine. Mars continues in Pisces and will hopefully bring some rain.

Northern Transplanting Time
July 19 to Aug 1 3ᵃ and
Aug 15 7ₚ to Aug 28 8ᵃ
Southern Transplanting Time
Aug 1 7ᵃ to Aug 15 3ₚ and
Aug 28 12ₚ to Sep 11

Harvest **seeds of fruit plants** and **grain** to be used for seed from Aug 18 9ᵃ to Aug 20 5ₚ, and at other Fruit times, avoiding unfavorable times.
   Immediately after harvest, sow catch crops like lupins, phacelia, mustard or wild flax.
   Seeds for leaf plants: harvest at Leaf times, specially in the second half of the month.
   Seeds for flower plants: at Flower times, specially in the second half of the month.

Burn **fly papers** in the cow barn at Flower times.
   Ants In the house: burn when the Moon is in Leo, Aug 18 9ᵃ to Aug 20 5ₚ.

Biodynamic preparations
Maria Thun's tree log preparations: Put birch and yarrow into the ground on Aug 25 between 4ₚ and 12ᵃ.

Aug

Unfavorable time

Date	Const. of Moon	Solar & lunar aspects	Moon Trines	El'ment	Parts of the plant enhanced by Moon or planets	Weather

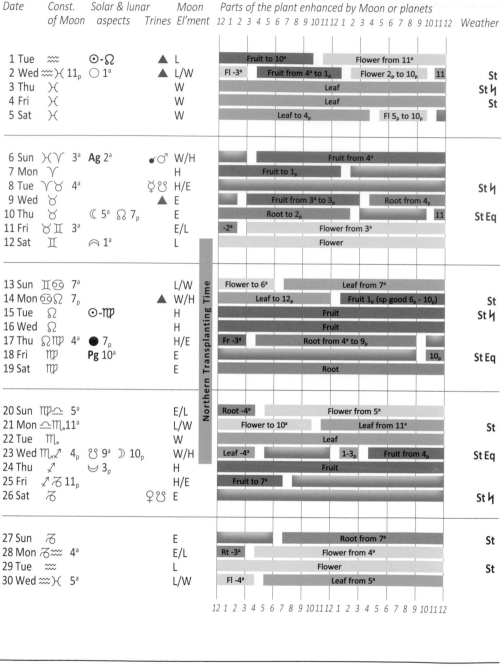

Date	Const. of Moon	Solar & lunar aspects	Trines	El'ment	Parts of the plant	Weather
1 Tue	♒	☉-♌	▲	L	Fruit to 10ᵃ / Flower from 11ᵃ	
2 Wed	♒♓ 11ₚ	○ 1ᵃ	▲	L/W	Fl -3ᵃ, Fruit from 4ᵃ to 1ₚ, Flower 2ₚ to 10ₚ, 11	St
3 Thu	♓			W	Leaf	St ♄
4 Fri	♓			W	Leaf	St
5 Sat	♓			W	Leaf to 4ₚ, Fl 5ₚ to 10ₚ	
6 Sun	♓♈ 3ᵃ	**Ag 2ᵃ**	☌♂	W/H	Fruit from 4ᵃ	
7 Mon	♈			H	Fruit to 1ₚ	
8 Tue	♈♉ 4ᵃ	☿☊		H/E		St ♄
9 Wed	♉		▲	E	Fruit from 3ᵃ to 3ₚ, Root from 4ₚ	
10 Thu	♉	☽ 5ᵃ ☋ 7ₚ		E	Root to 2ₚ, 11	St Eq
11 Fri	♉♊ 3ᵃ			E/L	-2ᵃ, Flower from 3ᵃ	
12 Sat	♊	☾ 1ᵃ		L	Flower	
13 Sun	♊♋ 7ᵃ			L/W	Flower to 6ᵃ, Leaf from 7ᵃ	
14 Mon	♋♌ 7ₚ		▲	W/H	Leaf to 12ₚ, Fruit 1ₚ (sp good 6ₚ - 10ₚ)	St
15 Tue	♌	☉-♍		H	Fruit	St ♄
16 Wed	♌			H	Fruit	
17 Thu	♌♍ 4ᵃ	● 7ₚ		H/E	Fr -3ᵃ, Root from 4ᵃ to 9ₚ	
18 Fri	♍	**Pg 10ᵃ**		E	10ₚ	St Eq
19 Sat	♍			E	Root	
20 Sun	♍♎ 5ᵃ			E/L	Root -4ᵃ, Flower from 5ᵃ	
21 Mon	♎♏ 11ᵃ			L/W	Flower to 10ᵃ, Leaf from 11ᵃ	St
22 Tue	♏			W	Leaf	
23 Wed	♏♐ 4ₚ	☋ 9ᵃ ☽ 10ₚ		W/H	Leaf -4ᵃ, 1-3ₚ, Fruit from 4ₚ	St Eq
24 Thu	♐	☉ 3ₚ		H	Fruit	
25 Fri	♐♑ 11ₚ			H/E	Fruit to 7ₚ	
26 Sat	♑	♀☊		E		St ♄
27 Sun	♑			E	Root from 7ᵃ	St
28 Mon	♑♒ 4ᵃ			E/L	Rt -3ᵃ, Flower from 4ᵃ	
29 Tue	♒			L	Flower	St
30 Wed	♒♓ 5ᵃ			L/W	Fl -4ᵃ, Leaf from 5ᵃ	

Northern Transplanting Time

12 1 2 3 4 5 6 7 8 9 10 11 12 1 2 3 4 5 6 7 8 9 10 11 12

Mercury ☿	Venus ♀	Mars ♂	Jupiter ♃	Saturn ♄	Uranus ♅	Neptune ♆	Pluto ♇
1 ♍	♊ 04 ♋	♓	♐	♐	♈	♒	♐
	22 ♌	(9 R)	(R 12 D)	(R 29 D)	(R)	(R)	(R)

NB: All zodiac symbols refer to astronomical constellations, not astrological signs (see p. 22)

Planetary aspects
(**Bold** = *visible to naked eye*)

1	☿△♇ 7ᵃ
2	♀♂♄ 8ᵃ ☉△♋ 10ᵃ ☾♂♆ 8ₚ
3	☿△♄ 3ᵃ ☾♂☿ 9ᵃ
4	
5	
6	☾♂♂ 1ᵃ
7	☾♂♋ 2ᵃ
8	☿☍ 2ₚ
9	☉△♃ 12ₚ
10	
11	☉♂♆ 4ₚ
12	☾♂♃ 1ₚ ☾♂♇ 10ᵤ
13	☾♂♄ 4ᵃ
14	☾♂♀ 3ᵈ ☉△♇ /ₚ
15	
16	☾♂♆ 10ₚ
17	☉△♄ 6ₚ
18	☽♂☿ 10ₚ
19	☽♂♂ 10ᵃ
20	☽♂♋ 7ᵃ
21	
22	
23	
24	☿♂♂ 7ᵃ
25	☽♂♃ 3ᵃ ☽♂♇ 12ₚ ☽♂♄ 5ₚ
26	♀☍ 6ₚ
27	
28	☽♂♀ 1ᵃ ♀△♂ 9ₚ
29	
30	☽♂♆ 1ᵃ

There are four Warmth trines during the first half of the month. This and the fact that Jupiter, Saturn, Uranus and Pluto are in Warmth constellations will bring a warm start to the autumn. In the first few days of the month Venus moves into Cancer, and together with Mars' retrograde movement in Pisces, makes the likelihood of rain greater.

Northern Transplanting Time
Sep 12 3ᵃ to Sep 24 1ₚ
Southern Transplanting Time
Aug 28 to Sep 11 11ₚ and
Sep 24 5ₚ to Oct 9

The times recommended for the **fruit harvest** are those in which the Moon is in Aries or Sagittarius (Sep 6 3ᵃ to Sep 7 1ₚ, Sep 23 4ₚ to Sep 25 7ᵃ) or other Fruit times.

The harvest of **root crops** is always best undertaken at Root times. Storage trials of onions, carrots, beetroot and potatoes have demonstrated this time and again.

Good times for **sowing winter grain** are when the Moon is in Leo or Sagittarius (Sep 14 7ₚ to Sep 17 3ᵃ, and Sep 23 4ₚ to Sep 25 7ᵃ) avoiding unfavorable times, and at other Fruit times.

Rye can if necessary also be sown at Root times with all subsequent cultivations being carried out at Fruit times.

Control slugs by burning between Sep 13 7ᵃ and Sep 14 6ₚ.

Planet (naked eye) visibility
Evening:
All night: Mars, Jupiter, Saturn
Morning: Venus

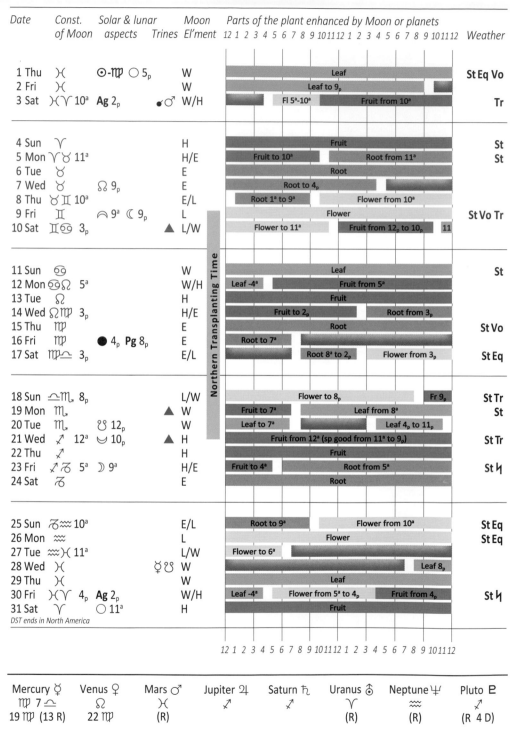

Date	Const. of Moon	Solar & lunar aspects	Moon Trines	El'ment	Parts of the plant enhanced by Moon or planets	Weather
1 Thu	♓	☉-♍ ○ 5ₚ		W	Leaf	St Eq Vo
2 Fri	♓			W	Leaf to 9ₚ	
3 Sat	♓♈ 10ᵃ	**Ag** 2ₚ	● ♂	W/H	Fl 5ᵃ-10ᵃ Fruit from 10ᵃ	Tr
4 Sun	♈			H	Fruit	St
5 Mon	♈♉ 11ᵃ			H/E	Fruit to 10ᵃ Root from 11ᵃ	St
6 Tue	♉			E	Root	
7 Wed	♉	♌ 9ₚ		E	Root to 4ₚ	
8 Thu	♉♊ 10ᵃ			E/L	Root 1ᵃ to 9ᵃ Flower from 10ᵃ	
9 Fri	♊	♐ 9ᵃ ☾ 9ₚ		L	Flower	St Vo Tr
10 Sat	♊♋ 3ₚ		▲	L/W	Flower to 11ᵃ Fruit from 12ₚ to 10ₚ 11	
11 Sun	♋			W	Leaf	St
12 Mon	♋♌ 5ᵃ			W/H	Leaf -4ᵃ Fruit from 5ᵃ	
13 Tue	♌			H	Fruit	
14 Wed	♌♍ 3ₚ			H/E	Fruit to 2ₚ Root from 3ₚ	
15 Thu	♍			E	Root	St Vo
16 Fri	♍	● 4ₚ **Pg** 8ₚ		E	Root to 7ᵃ	
17 Sat	♍♎ 3ₚ			E/L	Root 8ᵃ to 2ₚ Flower from 3ₚ	St Eq
18 Sun	♎♏ 8ₚ			L/W	Flower to 8ₚ Fr 9ₚ	St Tr
19 Mon	♏		▲	W	Fruit to 7ᵃ Leaf from 8ᵃ	St
20 Tue	♏	☍ 12ₚ		W	Leaf to 7ᵃ Leaf 4ₚ to 11ₚ	
21 Wed	♐ 12ᵃ	☌ 10ₚ	▲	H	Fruit from 12ᵃ (sp good from 11ᵃ to 9ₚ)	St Tr
22 Thu	♐			H	Fruit	
23 Fri	♐♑ 5ᵃ	☽ 9ᵃ		H/E	Fruit to 4ᵃ Root from 5ᵃ	St ♄
24 Sat	♑			E	Root	
25 Sun	♑♒ 10ᵃ			E/L	Root to 9ᵃ Flower from 10ᵃ	St Eq
26 Mon	♒			L	Flower	St Eq
27 Tue	♒♓ 11ᵃ			L/W	Flower to 6ᵃ	
28 Wed	♓	☿ ☍		W	Leaf 8ₚ	
29 Thu	♓			W	Leaf	
30 Fri	♓♈ 4ₚ	**Ag** 2ₚ		W/H	Leaf -4ᵃ Flower from 5ᵃ to 4ₚ Fruit from 4ₚ	St ♄
31 Sat	♈	○ 11ᵃ		H	Fruit	

DST ends in North America

Northern Transplanting Time

12 1 2 3 4 5 6 7 8 9 10 11 12 1 2 3 4 5 6 7 8 9 10 11 12

Mercury ☿	Venus ♀	Mars ♂	Jupiter ♃	Saturn ♄	Uranus ♅	Neptune ♆	Pluto ♇
♍ 7 ♎	♌	♓	♐	♐	♈	♒	♐
19 ♍ (13 R)	22 ♍	(R)			(R)	(R)	(R 4 D)

NB: All zodiac symbols refer to astronomical constellations, not astrological signs (see p. 22)

Planetary aspects
(**Bold** = *visible to naked eye*)

October 2020

1
2
3 ☾☌♂ 1ᵃ

4 ☾☍☿ 1ᵃ ☾☌♁ 7ᵃ
5
6
7 ☿☍♁ 5ₚ
8
9 ☾☌♃ 11ₚ
10 ☾☍♇ 7ᵃ ☾☍♄ 12ₚ ♀△♁ 7ₚ

11
12
13 ☉☍♂ 7ₚ ☾☌♀ 11ₚ
14 ☾☌♅ 0ᵃ
15
16 ☾☍♂ 10ᵃ
17 ☽☍♁ 4ₚ ☽☌☿ 6ₚ

18 ♀☍♆ 11ᵃ
19 ♀△♃ 4ᵃ ☿☍♁ 11ₚ
20
21 ♀△♇ 6ₚ
22 ☽☌♃ 2ₚ ☽☌♇ 7ₚ
23 ☽☌♄ 1ᵃ
24 ☿△♄ 12ₚ

25 ☉☌☿ 2ₚ
26
27 ☽☌♆ 6ᵃ
28 ☽☍♀ 6ᵃ ☿☊ 7ᵃ
29 ☽☌♂ 3ₚ
30 ☽☍☿ 12ₚ
31 ☽☌♁ 11ᵃ ☉☍♁ 12ₚ

Jupiter, Saturn, Uranus and Pluto remain in Warmth constellations, reinforced by three Warmth trines. In the last third of the month Mercury and Venus in the cool Earth constellation of Virgo may allow some cold weather.

Northern Transplanting Time
Oct 9 11ᵃ to Oct 21 8ₚ
Southern Transplanting Time
Sep 24 to Oct 9 7ᵃ and
Oct 22 1ᵃ to Nov 5

Store fruit at any Fruit or Flower time outside transplanting time.

Harvest seeds of root plants at Root times, **seeds for leaf plants** at Leaf times, and **seeds for flower plants** at Flower times.

All **cleared ground** should be treated with compost and sprayed with barrel preparation, and plowed ready for winter.

Control slugs by burning between Oct 10 3ₚ and Oct 12 4ᵃ.

Planet (naked eye) visibility
Evening: Jupiter, Saturn
All night: Mars
Morning: Mercury (from 31st), Venus

Oct

Unfavorable time

All times in EST

Date	Const. of Moon	Solar & lunar aspects	Moon Trines	El'ment	Parts of the plant enhanced by Moon or planets	Weather

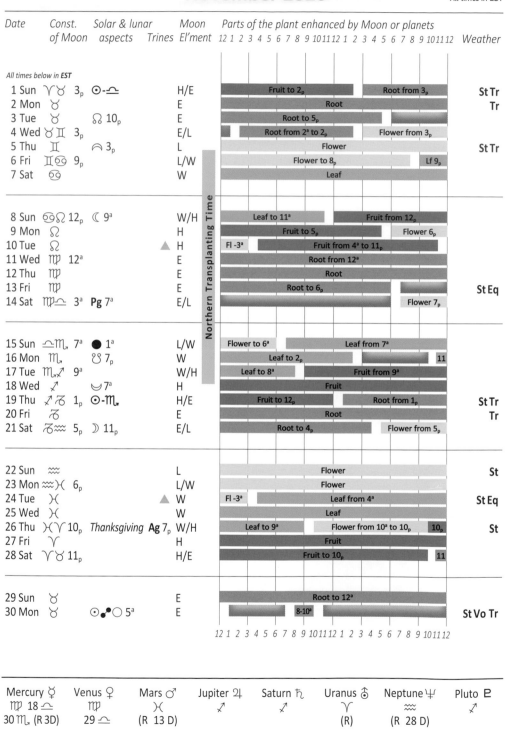

All times below in EST

1 Sun	♈♉ 3ₚ	☉-♎	H/E	Fruit to 2ₚ ... Root from 3ₚ — St Tr
2 Mon	♉		E	Root — Tr
3 Tue	♉	♌ 10ₚ	E	Root to 5ₚ
4 Wed	♉♊ 3ₚ		E/L	Root from 2ᵃ to 2ₚ ... Flower from 3ₚ
5 Thu	♊	⌒ 3ₚ	L	Flower — St Tr
6 Fri	♊♋ 9ₚ		L/W	Flower to 8ₚ ... Lf 9ₚ
7 Sat	♋		W	Leaf

Northern Transplanting Time

8 Sun	♋♌ 12ₚ	☽ 9ᵃ	W/H	Leaf to 11ᵃ ... Fruit from 12ₚ
9 Mon	♌		H	Fruit to 5ₚ ... Flower 6ₚ
10 Tue	♌	▲	H	Fl -3ᵃ ... Fruit from 4ᵃ to 11ₚ
11 Wed	♍ 12ᵃ		E	Root from 12ᵃ
12 Thu	♍		E	Root
13 Fri	♍		E	Root to 6ₚ — St Eq
14 Sat	♍♎ 3ᵃ	**Pg** 7ᵃ	E/L	Flower 7ₚ

15 Sun	♎♏ 7ᵃ	● 1ᵃ	L/W	Flower to 6ᵃ ... Leaf from 7ᵃ
16 Mon	♏	♋ 7ₚ	W	Leaf to 2ₚ ... 11
17 Tue	♏♐ 9ᵃ		W/H	Leaf to 8ᵃ ... Fruit from 9ᵃ
18 Wed	♐	⌣ 7ᵃ	H	Fruit
19 Thu	♐♑ 1ₚ	☉-♏	H/E	Fruit to 12ₚ ... Root from 1ₚ — St Tr
20 Fri	♑		E	Root — Tr
21 Sat	♑♒ 5ₚ	☽ 11ₚ	E/L	Root to 4ₚ ... Flower from 5ₚ

22 Sun	♒		L	Flower — St
23 Mon	♒♓ 6ₚ		L/W	Flower
24 Tue	♓	▲	W	Fl -3ᵃ ... Leaf from 4ᵃ — St Eq
25 Wed	♓		W	Leaf
26 Thu	♓♈ 10ₚ	*Thanksgiving* **Ag** 7ₚ	W/H	Leaf to 9ᵃ ... Flower from 10ᵃ to 10ₚ ... 10ₚ — St
27 Fri	♈		H	Fruit
28 Sat	♈♉ 11ₚ		H/E	Fruit to 10ₚ ... 11

29 Sun	♉		E	Root to 12ᵃ
30 Mon	♉	☉ ♂○ 5ᵃ	E	8-10ᵃ — St Vo Tr

Mercury ☿	Venus ♀	Mars ♂	Jupiter ♃	Saturn ♄	Uranus ♅	Neptune ♆	Pluto ♇
♍ 18 ♎	♍	♓	♐	♐	♈	♒	♐
30 ♏ (R 3D)	29 ♎	(R 13 D)			(R)	(R 28 D)	

NB: All zodiac symbols refer to astronomical constellations, not astrological signs (see p. 22)

Nov

    (**Bold** = *visible to naked eye*)

Jupiter, Saturn, Uranus and Pluto continue in Warmth constellations, there are two Light trines which, with Neptune in Aquarius and Mercury in Libra in the last two weeks of the month, will at least ensure some brightness.

1	
2	
3	
4	
5	
6	☾☌♃ 11^a ☾☌♇ 1_p ☾☌♄ 8_p
7	
8	
9	♀☌♂ 11^a
10	☉△♆ 1^a ☾☌♆ 4_p
11	
12	☾☌♂ 12_p ♃☌♇ 4_p ☾☌♀ 7_p
13	**☾☌☿ 5_p**
14	☾☍♁ 1^a
15	
16	
17	☿☍♁ 3^a
18	
19	☽☌♇ 3^a ☽☌♃ 5^a ☽☌♄ 11^a
20	
21	
22	
23	☽☌♆ 11^a
24	☿△♆ 1^a
25	☽☌♂ 7_p
26	
27	♀☍♁ 12_p ☽☍♀ 2_p ☽☌♁ 2_p
28	
29	☽☍☿ 4^a
30	

Northern Transplanting Time
Nov 5 5_p to Nov 18 5^a
Southern Transplanting Time
Oct 22 to Nov 5 1_p and
Nov 18 9^a to Dec 2

The Flower times in Transplanting Time are ideal for **planting flower bulbs,** showing vigorous growth and vivid colors. The remaining Flower times should only be considered as back up, as bulbs planted on those times will not flower so freely.

If not already completed in October, all organic waste materials should be gathered and made into a **compost.** Applying the biodynamic preparations to the compost will ensure a rapid transformation and good fungal development. An application of barrel preparation will also help the composting process.

Fruit and forest trees will also benefit at this time from a spraying of horn manure and/ or barrel preparation when being transplanted.

Best times for **cutting Advent greenery** and **Christmas trees** for transporting are Flower times, avoiding unfavorable times.

Burn **fly papers** in cow barn at Flower times.

Planet (naked eye) visibility
Evening: Jupiter, Saturn
All night: Mars
Morning: Mercury (to 29th), Venus

       Unfavorable time

December 2020

Date	Const. of Moon	Solar & lunar aspects	Trines	Moon El'ment	Parts of the plant enhanced by Moon or planets	Weather

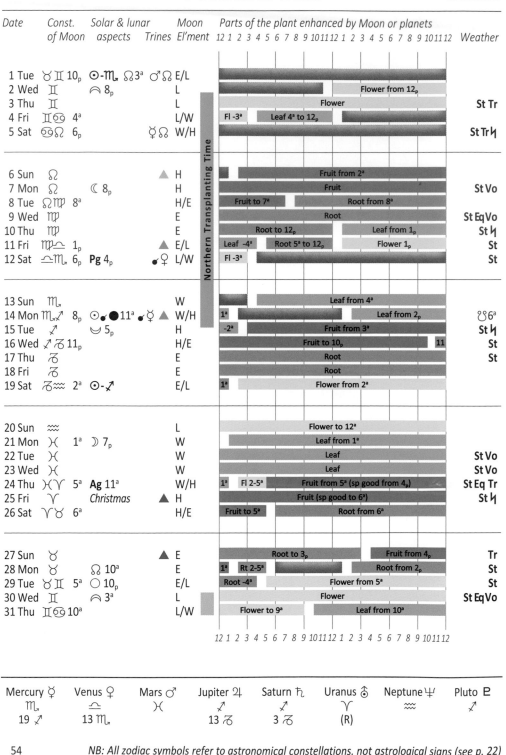

1 Tue ♉Ⅱ 10ₚ ☉-♏ ♌3ᵃ ♂♌ E/L
2 Wed Ⅱ ⌒ 8ₚ L — Flower from 12ₚ
3 Thu Ⅱ L — Flower — **St Tr**
4 Fri Ⅱ♋ 4ᵃ L/W — Fl -3ᵃ / Leaf 4ᵃ to 12ₚ — **St Tr ♄**
5 Sat ♋♌ 6ₚ ☿♌ W/H — **St Tr ♄**

6 Sun ♌ ▲ H — Fruit from 2ᵃ
7 Mon ♌ ☾ 8ₚ H — Fruit — **St Vo**
8 Tue ♌♍ 8ᵃ H/E — Fruit to 7ᵃ / Root from 8ᵃ — **St Eq Vo**
9 Wed ♍ E — Root — **St Eq Vo**
10 Thu ♍ E — Root to 12ₚ / Leaf from 1ₚ — **St ♄**
11 Fri ♍♎ 1ₚ ▲ E/L — Leaf -4ᵃ / Root 5ᵃ to 12ₚ / Flower 1ₚ — **St**
12 Sat ♎♏ 6ₚ **Pg** 4ₚ ○♀ L/W — Fl -3ᵃ — **St**

13 Sun ♏ W — Leaf from 4ᵃ
14 Mon ♏♐ 8ₚ ☉●11ᵃ ☿ ▲ W/H — 1ᵃ / Leaf from 2ₚ — ♋6ᵃ
15 Tue ♐ ⌣ 5ₚ H — -2ᵃ / Fruit from 3ᵃ — **St ♄**
16 Wed ♐♑ 11ₚ H/E — Fruit to 10ₚ / 11 — **St**
17 Thu ♑ E — Root — **St**
18 Fri ♑ E — Root
19 Sat ♑♒ 2ᵃ ☉-♐ E/L — 1ᵃ / Flower from 2ᵃ

20 Sun ♒ L — Flower to 12ᵃ
21 Mon ♓ 1ᵃ ☽ 7ₚ W — Leaf from 1ᵃ
22 Tue ♓ W — Leaf — **St Vo**
23 Wed ♓ W — Leaf — **St Vo**
24 Thu ♓♈ 5ᵃ **Ag** 11ᵃ W/H — 1ᵃ / Fl 2-5ᵃ / Fruit from 5ᵃ (sp good from 4ₚ) — **St Eq Tr**
25 Fri ♈ *Christmas* ▲ H — Fruit (sp good to 6ᵃ) — **St ♄**
26 Sat ♈♉ 6ᵃ H/E — Fruit to 5ᵃ / Root from 6ᵃ

27 Sun ♉ ▲ E — Root to 3ₚ / Fruit from 4ₚ — **Tr**
28 Mon ♉ ♌ 10ᵃ E — 1ᵃ / Rt 2-5ᵃ / Root from 2ₚ — **St**
29 Tue ♉Ⅱ 5ᵃ ○ 10ₚ E/L — Root -4ᵃ / Flower from 5ᵃ — **St**
30 Wed Ⅱ ⌒ 3ᵃ L — Flower — **St Eq Vo**
31 Thu Ⅱ♋ 10ᵃ L/W — Flower to 9ᵃ / Leaf from 10ᵃ

Northern Transplanting Time

12 1 2 3 4 5 6 7 8 9 10 11 12 1 2 3 4 5 6 7 8 9 10 11 12

Mercury ☿	Venus ♀	Mars ♂	Jupiter ♃	Saturn ♄	Uranus ♅	Neptune ♆	Pluto ♇
♏	♎	♓	♐	♐	♈	♒	♐
19 ♐	13 ♏		13 ♑	3 ♑	(R)		

NB: All zodiac symbols refer to astronomical constellations, not astrological signs (see p. 22)

(see p. 22)

Dec

Planetary aspects
(**Bold** = *visible to naked eye*)

1 ♂ ☋ 11ₚ — 1 ♂☋ 11p
2
3 ☾ ☌ ♇ 7p
4 ☾ ☌ ♃ 2ª   ☾ ☌ ♄ 6ª
5 ☿ ☋ 1p

6 ♀ △ ♆ 1ª
7 ☾ ☌ ♆ 11p
8
9
10 ☾ ☌ ♂ 4ª
11 ☉ △ ♂ 1ª   ☾ ☌ ☋ 9ª
12 ☾ ● ♀ 4p

13
14 ☾ ● ☿ 6ª   ☿ △ ♂ 11p
15
16 ☽ ☌ ♇ 3p
17 ☽ ☌ ♃ 1ª   ☽ ☌ ♄ 1ª
18
19 ☉ ☌ ☿ 11p

20 ☽ ☌ ♆ 7p
21 ♃ ☌ ♄ 2p
22
23 ☽ ☌ ♂ 6ª
24 ☽ ☌ ☋ 8p
25 ☿ △ ☋ 2ª
26

27 ☉ △ ☋ 10p
28 ☽ ☌ ♀ 2ª
29
30 ☾ ☌ ☿ 11ª
31 ☾ ☌ ♇ 3ª   ☾ ☌ ♄ 5p   ☾ ☌ ♃ 7p

The first half of the month may be wet with two Water trines and Mercury in Scorpio and Mars in Pisces. Jupiter and Saturn move into the cold Earth constellation of Capricorn where their (only once very twenty years) conjunction is at the winter solstice. A white Christmas may be possible, though Mars and Venus in Watery constellations will have to counter the Warmth trine on Christmas Day.

Northern Transplanting Time
Dec 2 10ₚ to Dec 15 3ₚ and
Dec 30 5ª to Jan 12
Southern Transplanting Time
Nov 18 to Dec 2 6ₚ and
Dec 15 7ₚ to Dec 30 1ª

The transplanting time is good for **pruning trees and hedges.** Fruit trees should be pruned at Fruit or Flower times.

Best times for cutting **Advent greenery** and **Christmas trees** are at Flower times to ensure lasting fragrance.

Burn feathers or skins of **warm blooded pests** from Dec 26 6ª to Dec 27 3ₚ.

We wish all our readers a blessed festive time and the best of health for the New Year of 2021

Planet (naked eye) visibility
Evening: Mars, Jupiter, Saturn
All night:
Morning: Venus

Unfavorable time   55

Sowing times for trees and shrubs

July 27: Yew, Oak, Hornbeam, Cherry, Horse chestnut (buckeye), Sweet chestnut, Spruce, Fir

Aug 1: Alder, Larch, Lime tree, Elm, Juniper, Plum

Aug 3: Ash, Cedar, Fir, Spruce, Hazel, Lime tree, Elm, Thuja, Juniper, Plum, Hornbeam

Aug 26: Maple, Apple, Apricot, Birch, Pear, Hornbeam, Lime tree, Mirabelle plum, Peach, Plum, Robinia, Thuja, Juniper, Willow

Aug 30 (before 5_p): Birch, Pear, Lime tree, Robinia, Willow, Thuja, Juniper, Plum, Hornbeam

Sep 2: Pear, Birch, Lime tree, Robinia, Willow, Thuja, Juniper, Plum, Hornbeam

Sep 11: Ash, Spruce, Hazel, Fir, Cedar

Oct 7: Alder, Larch, Lime tree, Elm

Oct 31: Ash, Cedar, Fir, Spruce, Hazel

Sowing times depend on planetary aspects and are not specific to either northern or southern hemispheres. For trees and shrubs not mentioned above, sow at an appropriate time of the Moon's position in the zodiac, depending on the part of the tree or shrub to be enhanced. Avoid unfavorable times.

Sowing times are different from transplanting times. Seedlings should be transplanted during the descending Moon when the Moon is in a constellation corresponding to the part of the tree to to be enhanced. It is important to remember that seedlings need to sufficiently mature to withstand the winter. The time of sowing should therefore chime in with local conditions and take account of the germination habit of each tree species.

Felling times for timber

March 28: Birch, Pear, Robinia, Willow, Maple, Apple, Copper beech, Sweet chestnut, Walnut

May 17: Ash, Spruce, Hazel, Fir, Cedar

July 30: Alder, Larch, Lime tree, Elm

Aug 25: Alder, Larch, Lime tree, Elm, Birch, Pear, Robinia, Willow, Maple, Apple, Copper beech, Sweet chestnut, Walnut

Sep 2: Ash, Spruce, Hazel, Fir, Cedar

Sep 9 (from 9^a): Ash, Spruce, Hazel, Fir, Cedar

Oct 11: Birch, Pear, Larch, Lime tree, Robinia, Willow

Oct 29: Birch, Pear, Robinia, Willow, Maple, Apple, Copper beech, Sweet chestnut, Walnut

Nov 24: Alder, Larch, Lime tree, Elm

Dec 25: Alder, Larch, Lime tree, Elm, Birch, Pear, Robinia, Willow, Maple, Apple, Copper beech, Sweet chestnut, Walnut

Dec 28 (after 1_p): Ash, Spruce, Hazel, Fir, Cedar

Those trees which are not listed should be felled at the end of the growing season at Flower times during the descending Moon period (transplanting time). Avoid unfavorable times.

A recipe for rye bread

Since all the grains we grow in our experiments were tested for quality, we have used our own raising agents (without additives) for bread baking to produce a good loaf. Besides sour milk, buttermilk, whey and syrup we have also tried to bake with honey and have developed a recipe that has proved its worth over many years.

To make 2 large loafs, use 4 lb (2 kg) of rye flour.

One heaped teaspoon of flower honey is stirred well in a glass of warm water (120°F, 50°C) and then mixed with ¼ lb (125 g) of finely-ground rye flour. This small amount of dough is made in the evening and kept warm overnight to allow it to rise for the first time. It should be at a temperature of about 80–85°F (26–30°C) by the stove or next to a hot plate, which is set very low. Next morning, add the same amount of rye flour and warm water or whey and allow to rise for the second time.

In the evening, add just over 2 lb (1 kg) of the flour to the prepared dough with sufficient warm water. At this stage you can add a little linseed, caraway, fennel or something similar. After mixing in these herbs, add the rest of the flour. Leave it to rise overnight for the third time. Next morning, add salt and knead the dough. When it begins to rise for the fourth time the dough is ready.

Put some finished dough aside to use as a starter for next time. Shape the loaves, let them rise well, put them in a preheated oven (300°F, 150°C). After ten minutes increase the temperature to 390°F (200°C), and bake them for another 50 minutes. Check the loaves; as every oven is a bit different, the time may vary. Rye is easy to digest when it has gone through these five stages.

Keep the starter in an earthenware pot. After it has risen again a little, sprinkle with salt, cover with grease-proof paper and store in a cool place (not the fridge). When you want to do some more baking, take the pot from the cool place in the morning and add a teaspoon of honey, which has been stirred in a glass of warm water. Then keep the pot warm. In the evening you can start on the main dough and proceed as described above.

Traditionally after 40 days, the starter was no longer used, and the process was started from stage one again.

Rye should rise five times. Wheat, barley and oats need to rise only three times. Success depends on the warmth of the baking area.

The care of bees

A colony of bees lives in its hive closed off from the outside world. For extra protection against harmful influences, the inside of the hive is sealed with propolis. The link with the wider surroundings is made by the bees that fly in and out of the hive.

To make good use of cosmic rhythms, the beekeeper needs to create the right conditions in much the same way as the gardener or farmer does with the plants. The gardener works the soil and in so doing allows cosmic forces to penetrate it via the air. These forces can then be taken up and used by the plants until the soil is next moved.

When the beekeeper opens up the hive, the sealing layer of propolis is broken. This creates a disturbance, as a result of which cosmic forces can enter and influence the life of the hive until the next intervention by the beekeeper. By this means the beekeeper can directly mediate cosmic forces to the bees.

It is not insignificant which forces of the universe are brought into play when the the hive is opened. The beekeeper can consciously intervene by choosing days for working with the hive that will help the colony to develop and build up its food reserves. The bees will then reward the beekeeper by providing a portion of their harvest in the form of honey.

Earth-Root times can be selected for opening the hive if the bees need to do more building. *Light-Flower* times encourage brood activity and colony development. *Warmth-Fruit* times stimulate the collection of nectar. *Water-Leaf* times are unsuitable for working in the hive or for the removal and processing of honey.

Since the late 1970s the varroa mite has affected virtually every bee colony in Europe. Following a number of comparative trials we recommend burning and making an ash of the varroa mite in the usual way. After dynamizing it for one hour, the ash should be put in a salt-cellar and sprinkled lightly between the combs. The ash should be made and sprinkled when the Sun and Moon are in Taurus (May/June).

Over the years I have come to sprinkle small amounts of ash on the brood to strengthen its effect whenever I carry out an inspection.

Spraying the varroa ash using a salt-celler.

Fungal problems

The function of fungus in nature is to break down dying organic materials. It appears amongst our crops when unripe manure compost or uncomposted animal by-products such as horn and bone meal are used but also when seeds are harvested during unfavorable constellations: according to Steiner, 'When Moon forces are working too strongly on the Earth ...'

Tea can be made from horsetail (*Equisetum arvense*) and sprayed on to the soil where affected plants are growing. This draws the fungal level back down into the ground where it belongs.

The plants can be strengthened by spraying stinging nettle tea on the leaves. This will promote good assimilation, stimulate the flow of sap and help fungal diseases to disappear.

Biodynamic preparation plants

Pick dandelions in the morning at Flower times as soon as they are open and while the center of the flowers are still tightly packed.

Pick yarrow at Fruit times when the Sun is in Leo (around the middle of August).

Pick camomile at Flower times just before midsummer. If they are harvested too late, seeds will begin to form and there are often grubs in the hollow heads.

Collect stinging nettles when the first flowers are opening, usually around midsummer. Harvest the whole plants without roots at Flower times.

Pick valerian at Flower times around midsummer.

All the flowers (except valerian) should be laid out on paper and dried in the shade.

Collect oak bark at Root times. The pithy material below the bark should not be used.

Moon diagrams

The diagrams overleaf show for each month the daily position (evenings GMT) of the Moon against the stars and other planets. For viewing in the southern hemisphere, turn the diagrams upside down.

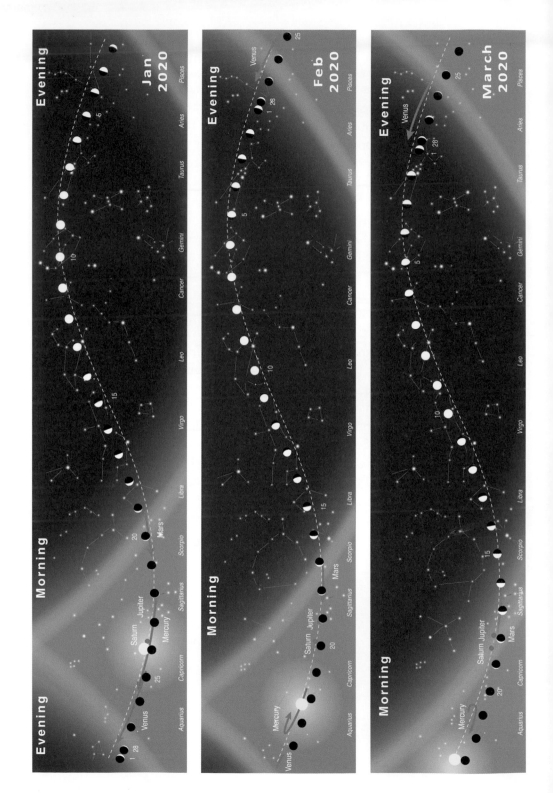

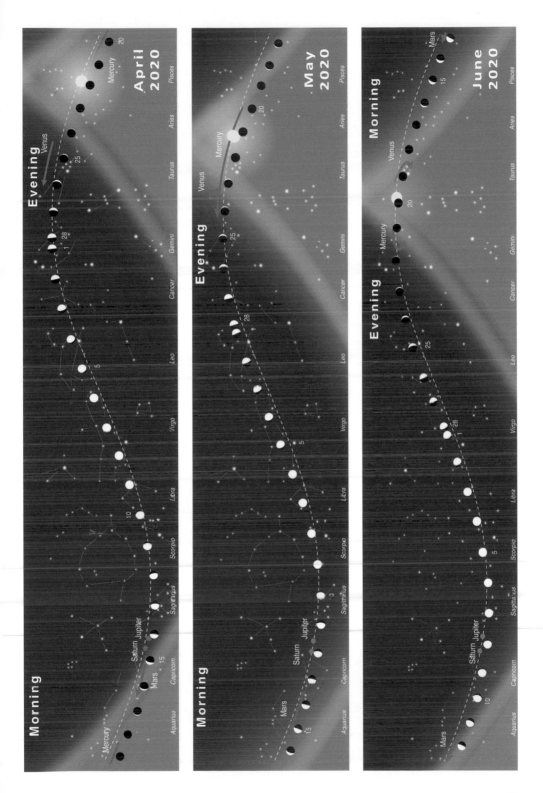

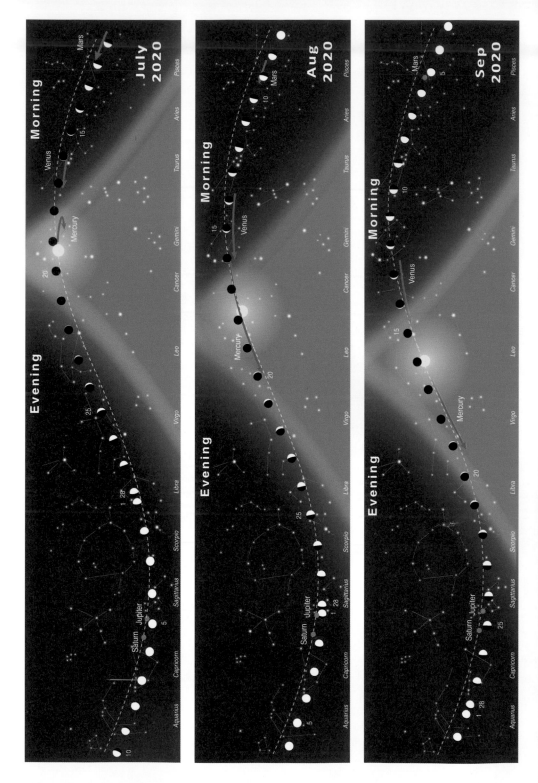

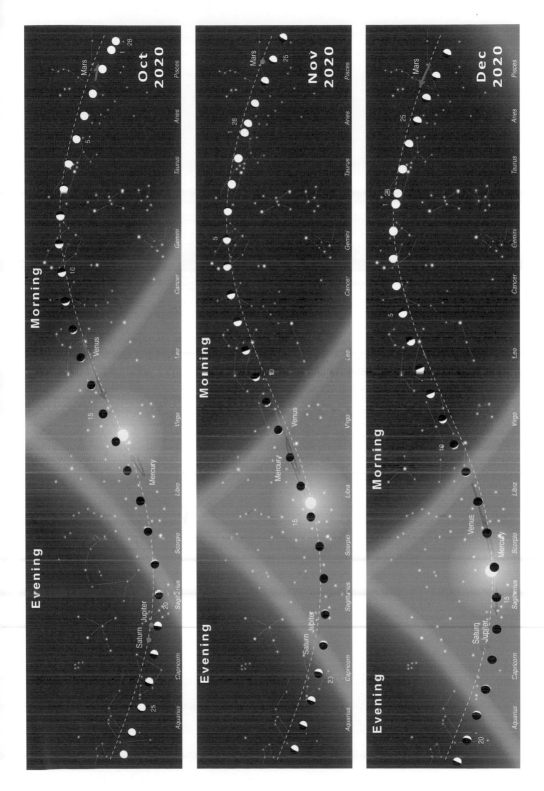

Further Reading

Berrevoets, Erik, *Wisdom of Bees: Principles of Biodynamic Beekeeping,* SteinerBooks, USA

Colquhoun, Margaret and Axel Ewald, *New Eyes for Plants,* Hawthorn

Karlsson, Britt and Per, *Biodynamic, Organic and Natural Winemaking,* Floris

Klett, Manfred, *Principles of Biodynamic Spray and Compost Preparations,* Floris

Klocek, Dennis, *Sacred Agriculture: The Alchemy of Biodynamics,* Lindisfarne

Koepf, H.H., *The Biodynamic Farm: Agriculture in the Service of Humanity,* SteinerBooks, USA

—, *Koepf's Practical Biodynamics: Soil, Compost, Sprays and Food Quality,* Floris

König, Karl, *Social Farming: Healing Humanity and the Earth,* Floris

Kranich, Ernst Michael, *Planetary Influences upon Plants,* Biodynamic Association, USA

Lepetit, Antoine, *What's so Special About Biodynamic Wine?* Floris

Masson, Pierre, *A Biodynamic Manual,* Floris

Morrow, Joel, *Vegetable Gardening for Organic and Biodynamic Growers,* Lindisfarne

Osthaus, K.-E., *The Biodynamic Farm,* Floris

Pfeiffer, Ehrenfried, *The Earth's Face,* Lanthorn

—, *Pfeiffer's Introduction to Biodynamics,* Floris

—, *Weeds and What They Tell Us,* Floris

—, & Michael Maltas, *The Biodynamic Orchard Book,* Floris

Philbrick, John and Helen, *Gardening for Health and Nutrition,* Anthroposophic, USA

Philbrick, Helen & Gregg, Richard B., *Companion Plants and How to Use Them,* Floris

Sattler, Friedrich & Eckard von Wistinghausen, *Growing Biodynamic Crops,* Floris

Schilthuis, Willy, *Biodynamic Agriculture,* Floris

Selg, Peter, *The Agricultural Course: Rudolf Steiner and the Beginnings of Biodynamics,* Temple Lodge

Steiner, Rudolf, *Agriculture (A Course of Eight Lectures),* Biodynamic Association, USA

—, *Agriculture: An Introductory Reader,* Steiner Press, UK

—, *What is Biodynamics? A Way to Heal and Revitalize the Earth,* SteinerBooks, USA

Storl, Wolf, *Culture and Horticulture,* North Atlantic Books, USA

Thun, Maria, *Gardening for Life,* Hawthorn

—, *The Biodynamic Year,* Temple Lodge

Thun, Matthias, *When Wine Tastes Best: A Biodynamic Calendar for Wine Drinkers,* (annual) Floris

von Keyserlink, Adelbert Count, *The Birth of a New Agriculture,* Temple Lodge

—, *Developing Biodynamic Agriculture,* Temple Lodge

Weiler, Michael, *The Secret of Bees: An Insider's Guide to the Life of the Honeybee,* Floris

Wright, Hilary, *Biodynamic Gardening for Health and Taste,* Floris

Biodynamic Associations

Demeter International
www.demeter.net

Australia:
Bio-Dynamic Research Institute
www.demeter.org.au
Biodynamic Agriculture Australia
www.biodynamics.net.au

Canada: Society for Bio-Dynamic Farming & Gardening in Ontario
biodynamics.on.ca

India: Bio-Dynamic Association of India (BDAI)
www.biodynamics.in

Ireland: Biodynamic Agriculture Association of Ireland
www.biodynamicagriculture.ie

New Zealand:
NZ Biodynamic Association
www.biodynamic.org.nz

South Africa: Biodynamic Agricultural Association of Southern Africa
www.bdaasa.org.za

UK: Biodynamic Association
www.biodynamic.org.uk

USA: Biodynamic Association
www.biodynamics.com